Advanced Introduction to Demography

Elgar Advanced Introductions are stimulating and thoughtful introductions to major fields in the social sciences, business and law, expertly written by the world's leading scholars. Designed to be accessible yet rigorous, they offer concise and lucid surveys of the substantive and policy issues associated with discrete subject areas.

The aims of the series are two-fold: to pinpoint essential principles of a particular field, and to offer insights that stimulate critical thinking. By distilling the vast and often technical corpus of information on the subject into a concise and meaningful form, the books serve as accessible introductions for undergraduate and graduate students coming to the subject for the first time. Importantly, they also develop well-informed, nuanced critiques of the field that will challenge and extend the understanding of advanced students, scholars and policy-makers.

For a full list of titles in the series please see the back of the book. Recent titles in the series include:

Legal Reasoning
Larry Alexander and Emily Sherwin

Sustainable Competitive Advantage in Sales
Lawrence B. Chonko

Law and Development
Second Edition
Mariana Mota Prado and Michael J. Trebilcock

Law and Renewable Energy
Joel B. Eisen

Marxism and Human Geography
Kevin R. Cox

Maritime Law
Paul Todd

American Foreign Policy
Loch K. Johnson

Water Politics
Ken Conca

Business Ethics
John Hooker

Employee Engagement
Alan M. Saks and Jamie A. Gruman

Governance
Jon Pierre and B. Guy Peters

Demography
Wolfgang Lutz

Advanced Introduction to

Demography

WOLFGANG LUTZ

Professor of Demography, Department of Demography, University of Vienna; Director, Vienna Institute of Demography, Austrian Academy of Sciences; Research Group Leader, International Institute for Applied Systems Analysis (IIASA), and Founding Director, Wittgenstein Centre for Demography and Global Human Capital (IIASA, OeAW, University of Vienna), Austria

Elgar Advanced Introductions

 Edward **Elgar**
PUBLISHING

Cheltenham, UK • Northampton, MA, USA

Published by
Edward Elgar Publishing Limited
The Lypiatts
15 Lansdown Road
Cheltenham
Glos GL50 2JA
UK

Edward Elgar Publishing, Inc.
William Pratt House
9 Dewey Court
Northampton
Massachusetts 01060
USA

A catalogue record for this book
is available from the British Library

Library of Congress Control Number: 2021943528

Printed on elemental chlorine free (ECF)
recycled paper containing 30% Post-Consumer Waste

ISBN 978 1 78990 146 7 (cased)
ISBN 978 1 78990 148 1 (paperback)
ISBN 978 1 78990 147 4 (eBook)
Printed and bound in the USA

Contents

Preface

"Demo…what?" was written in big letters on a T-shirt that I got from my friends at a farewell party in 1982, leaving the University of Pennsylvania with a degree in demography and heading back to Europe. And sure enough, nobody in Austria had a clue what demography was, most people thinking I said democracy. Today the situation is very different. The newspapers write about demography all the time, mostly with negative connotations about demographic threats and problems. The European Commission has a vice president with a specific portfolio on "Democracy and Demography", the German chancellor Merkel personally chaired the German "Demografie Initiative", while French president Macron has called demographic trends in Africa one of Europe's greatest challenges. Today, whenever I tell people what is my scientific discipline they tend to react by saying "Yes, demographic issues are the biggest problems we face, together with climate change".

I have mixed feelings about this new prominence of demography. On the one hand, I do not complain about more attention given to the small scientific discipline that I chose to be my field of studies over four decades ago. On the other hand, I feel that demography became more prominent for the wrong reasons. My research over the years clearly taught me that neither increases nor decreases in population size by themselves nor changing age structures necessarily bring big problems. Much depends on what people are able to do and willing to do. I understood that even as demographers we should not only focus on the headcount but also consider what is inside the heads, and that we have a powerful toolbox to address this issue quantitatively through the methods of multi-dimensional demography that differentiates by level of education and other cognition-based categories.

Acknowledgements

I would like to thank the following colleagues for helpful comments and suggestions on an early draft of the text, in particular on Chapter 2 on demographic theories: Alain Belanger, William P. Butz, Joel Cohen, David Coleman, Andreas Edel, Dalkhat Ediev, Marc Luy, Dimiter Philipov, Samuel H. Preston, and John R. Weeks.

I would also like to thank Stefanie Andruchowitz for help with editing the text and Claudia Reiter for work on the figures.

1 Demographic concepts and data

Foundations of demography

The date and place of birth of demography – unlike that of most other scientific disciplines – can be rather precisely defined. On February 5, 1661, John Graunt (1620–1674) presented 50 copies of his book entitled, *Natural and Political Observations Made Upon the Bills of Mortality* (Graunt, 1661) to the Royal Society in London. In this book he developed the basic statistical methods for estimating life tables and other demographic estimation methods based on censuses and counts of deaths and births, which essentially provided the basis for modern demography.

In the 17th and 18th centuries some of the leading mathematicians and philosophers, such as John Locke (1632–1704) and David Hume (1711–1776) were also interested in demographic questions. Edmund Halley (1656–1742) was an astronomer interested in demography, using data from Breslau to advance life table methods, and Leonhard Euler (1707–1783) developed most of the mathematical foundations of modern formal demography. However, the dominating figure in 18th-century empirical demography was the German pastor, Johann Peter Süssmilch (1707–1767), who published in 1741 and 1761–1762, *Die Göttliche Ordnung in den Veränderungen des menschlichen Geschlechts aus der Geburt, dem Tode und der Fortpflanzung desselben* (*The Divine Order with Regard to the Human Species, as Demonstrated by Birth, Death and Reproduction*) (Süssmilch, 1741). He looked for proof of a divine order in the regularity of demographic events and, in doing so, collected masses of empirical data from a great number of sources and thus provided material for the next generation of demographers, including Thomas Robert

Malthus (1766–1834). Malthus, in *An Essay on the Principle of Population* (Malthus, 1798) makes the point that otherwise exponential population growth is restricted by the slower growth of food supplies, an influential and controversial claim that is still being debated to this day. This view was in sharp contrast to the optimistic views of Marquis de Condorcet (1743–1794) who believed that continued education and female empowerment would solve most problems through behavioral and technological innovation. While this is not the place for providing a full history of the discipline of demography it is worth noting that the French astronomer Pierre Simon Laplace (1749–1827), the Belgian Adolphe Quetelet (1796–1874) and the German Wilhelm Lexis (1837–1914) also made important contributions to developing the methodology of an independent scientific discipline. The first international scientific organization of demographers was established in 1928 and later called International Union for the Scientific Study of Population (IUSSP).

Definition of demography

On its website (www.iussp.org), the IUSSP currently offers a set of different definitions of demography that differ somewhat in their emphasis but are in fact very similar. There is the definition given in Demopaedia (www.demopaedia.org), a website run by the IUSSP and the United Nations providing a multilingual demographic dictionary, which states: "Demography is the scientific study of human populations primarily with respect to their size, their structure and their development; it takes into account the quantitative aspects of their general characteristics." The IUSSP also lists more personal definitions by a number of distinguished demographers that all have in common that demography is a scientific discipline dealing with the human population and its changes in a quantitative/statistical way. The most concise and even classical definition, which until recently was the only one given on the IUSSP website, is that it is the *scientific study of changing population size and structures*. Personally, I prefer an even more general definition such as the *quantitative study of groups of people* or *the mathematics of groups of people*.

What most of these definitions have in common is that they refer to multiple demographic characteristics or population structures stated in plural. This implies the analysis of multiple demographic structures which, in addition to standard reference to age and sex, also include place of residence, level of education, labor force participation, ethnicity and others.

Historically these refer to the characteristics of individuals that have been typically collected in censuses or are often labeled as "demographics" as the standard background information collected in many surveys dealing with a range of different non-demographic topics. Since populations can be stratified by these characteristics, which can be plotted along an axis, they are also called demographic dimensions. If a population is stratified only by age, this is a one-dimensional model, if stratified by age and sex (the classic age pyramid as described in more detail below) the analysis can be called two-dimensional. If it considers three or more dimensions, it is called *multi-dimensional demographic analysis*. The age-, sex-, and education-pyramids frequently used in this volume are thus called either three-dimensional or multi-dimensional.

In some contexts, a narrower understanding of demography sees demographic change exclusively with respect to changes in the age structure of populations. When, in Europe, politicians or experts from other disciplines, such as economists, refer to demographic change, then what is often meant is primarily the changing age structure of the population, sometimes also differentiated by sex. While changes in the age structure are certainly highly relevant for many social and economic issues, there are also other highly relevant demographic dimensions. This overly narrow perspective on age and sex alone may have to do with the fact that many widely available population data and projections are often only presented by age and sex. If this is what demographers typically present to the rest of the world, then the rest of the world may think this is all we have to offer. For this reason, here I try to emphasize examples of demographic analysis and projections that go beyond age and sex.

The multi-dimensional understanding of demography underlying this volume is not only in line with the origin of the discipline and the writings of its most distinguished representatives, it also is in line with the way international media often write about demography. When they write about the changing demographics of, for example, the American electorate, they do not just mean the changing age composition but also the changing composition by ethnicity, rural/urban place of residence, educational attainment, occupational groups, etc.

Linguistically, the word demography is derived from the ancient Greek word "demos" which means the population, the aggregate of individuals living in a city state ("polis") together with "graphein" which means to write, draw or map (such as in geography). The word "demos" is the same word that is the basis for the more famous and better-known notion of democracy (the rule by the demos). While in ancient Greece this membership in the ruling demos was mostly restricted to free male citizens – thus leaving out all women, slaves and the so-called metics (landless migrants) – today demos is widely understood to include all citizens of both genders and all social groups. In ancient Greek political writing, the interests of the demos are often seen as opposed to that of the selfish individual "idiotes". There also is a verb "demotizo" which means moving something from the private to the public good, a word that had also been used in the sense of confiscation in the interest of the public. This linguistic background makes it very clear that the original meaning of demography is exclusively referring to the aggregate level, to changes at the macro-level of populations or societies.

Micro versus macro: individual life courses versus population changes

Demography deals with groups of individuals. As will be stated in Proposition 1 for the foundation of demographic theories in the following chapter, people – individual humans – are considered the primary building blocks of every population or sub-population of interest and the primary agents of social and economic behavior. Combined to groups of people they become a population – with clear definitions who belongs to a specified population and who does not – whose changes over time are the explicit focus of the science of demography as defined above.

Under this approach, people can be seen as the atoms of society, who act and interact with each other. Following this analogy, households – which particularly in economics are, more often than individuals, seen as the basic unit of analysis when it comes to decision making – may be viewed as molecules. This frequent focus on households in economic studies may also have to do with the fact that available data on income or consumption as derived from surveys typically provide household-level information without specifying the contributions of individual household members. This is based on the usual assumption that within each household resources are pooled and distributed on an equal basis. But there is abundant evidence that not all households are egalitarian and there may even be rather strong forms of inequality and exploitation. In most households there are differentiated needs and differentiated roles next higher level. Since in this example movements are only possible in one direction (towards higher educational attainment) such a model is also called a *hierarchical model*. At any point in time people can also leave the population through death, with death rates varying by education category in addition to age and sex. The balancing equation also holds for specific age groups and cohorts.

This fundamental demographic identity is comprehensive in the sense that there cannot be any other change in any clearly specified population between two points in time that is not caused by either births or deaths or movements in and out of the population (migrations or transitions to other categories/states). It is also exact in terms of not being an approximation. All terms in the equation are discrete natural numbers representing individual people being born, dying or moving between categories. If things do not add up using the empirical numbers of any real country, then this must be due to measurement error because, by definition, the identity given in formula (1) must hold. In practical terms, therefore, one of the most frequent applications of the identity is to estimate net migration (the balance of in- and out-migration) as the residual that remains unexplained when having reliable data of the population sizes (e.g. from censuses) for dates t and $t+1$ and births and deaths (from vital registration) over that period of time, but there is no reliable empirical data on migration.

In the context of the broader field of social sciences it is also worth noting that this fundamental demographic identity goes beyond the usual statistical study of associations. By being exact and holding over time and space for all different sub-population it gives demography a clear quantitative/mathematical structure that can also be used for forecasting and that distinguishes demography from most other social sciences.

Kenneth Boulding, who is widely considered the father of evolutionary economics and to some extent of ecological economics, saw this demographic balancing equation as most fundamental for a unified social science based on a general systems theory (Boulding, 1956; Preston et al., 2000). Boulding emphasized that human economic and other behavior is embedded in a larger system of social, economic and environmental factors and that individuals are, in a way, the "atoms" whose changing composition in a population interact with these environmental factors. The quantitative structure presented by this population-balancing equation provides demography with a sound mathematical basis for assessing trends and studying patterns over age and time (Arthur & Vaupel, 1983; Preston & Coale, 1982) not only for the past and present but also for studying the future. This puts demography in general and the population balancing equation in particular at the basis of much of modern quantitative social science, including economics.

Period and cohort perspectives

As explained in the previous section, demographic change results from the aggregation of individual life histories. Every individual life course starts with birth and ends with death. And the most frequently used metric for studying progress in the advance of the life course is age, typically measured as time since birth. To be more precise here, one should say "chronological age" since in recent years other concepts of age – such as biological age or age defined in terms of remaining life expectancy – have also been introduced (Sanderson & Scherbov, 2005). Chronological age is based on the same clock that also measures the passage of historical time. Under this definition the personal micro-time and the historical macro-time go at the same speed. They go in parallel, marching in step, or "pari passu" as said in Latin. This marching in step of age and time lies at the heart of much of the toolbox of demographic methods and analytical concepts.

The best way to visualize this parallel change in age and time for individual life courses as well as for groups of individuals is using the so-called Lexis diagram, named after the German mathematician and demographer, Wilhelm Lexis (1837–1914). It simply puts time on the horizontal axis and age on the vertical axis (Figure 1.2). Individual life courses are then lines at an angle of 45 degrees, starting at the date of birth, of a person who then becomes one year older every year. But the Lexis diagram is not only a good way of depicting the life courses of individuals. People can also be grouped into cohorts that were born in the same time interval. This standard definition of a cohort as a group of people that share the same timing of the initializing event (birth, or marriage in the case of marriage cohorts) as introduced by Norman Ryder (1965) will be further discussed in the context of the Demographic Metabolism Theory in Chapter 2. In Figure 1.2, birth cohort a is depicted as the group of people born in time period t, which is the period between A and C. This cohort of children will then reach age 1 during time period $t+1$ which will be between B and

D. As the chart also shows, some of the members of this cohort will have spent their first year of life primarily in time period *t* while others did so in period *t*+1. This is important to consider in demographic modeling when, for example, child mortality conditions are changing from period *t* to *t*+1.

Another advantage of the Lexis diagram is that it can help to illustrate the difference between the cohort perspective and the period perspective. While cohorts follow the diagonals, the period perspective in demography only looks at events happening within one time period, such as year *t*. The period perspective thus looks at the vertical block above *t* which, for the first age group, is the square as defined by the square A–C–B–E. For higher age groups in period *t* we look at the squares that are (vertically) above that lowest square. This period perspective is a very frequently taken approach in demography because data on demographic counts (number of people at different ages in a certain year) as well as vital events (deaths by age or births by age of mother in a given year) tend to come by calendar years. Hence, if we want to measure the child mortality rate of children below age 5 in year *t* we relate the child deaths that are measured as happening to children in the five squares above A–C to the number of person-years lived by all children in those five squares.

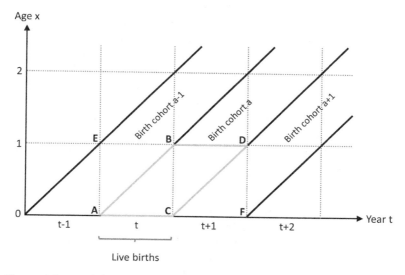

Figure 1.2   Schematic presentation of a Lexis diagram for selected birth cohorts

At this stage, the notion of "person years" that is central to the definition of demographic rates requires some explanation. The so-called occurrence-exposure rates want to relate the number of events in each age group in each period (such as deaths at age a in period t) to the number of persons exposed to the risk of mortality over the period. Since not all people who start the year t in the country considered will stay there for the whole year – some may die during the year, others may leave the country – the person years of exposure need to be adjusted for this. Hence, unlike in the case of a probability of transition which has in its denominator the initial full count of the starting population, a rate has in its denominator always the number of person years actually exposed to the risk of transition. In practice, this is often approximated by an estimate of the mid-year population.

Box 1.1   Period and cohort Total Fertility Rates (TFR)

The table below shows empirical age-specific fertility rates for 5-year age groups for Austria for the periods since 1980–85. The data give the number of births to women in the stated age groups for 1000 women of the age group that are exposed to the risk of birth.

The period Total Fertility Rates (P-TFR) for a given time period (columns in the table below) are calculated as the sum of the age-specific fertility rates multiplied by 5 because they refer to 5-year age groups. These P-TFRs can be interpreted as the average number of births born to a woman in the hypothetical (synthetic) cohort of women who experience at each age the age-specific fertility rates as measured in the given period. It thus is a summary measure of the fertility experience of a year or 5-year period.

The cohort Total Fertility Rate (C-TFR) is the sum of age-specific fertility rates along the diagonal since every real cohort of women will be five years older every five years. It thus covers the experience of women who were 15–19 years in 1980–85 and 45–49 years in 2010–15. The resulting pattern of TFRs also shows that the cohort fertility level is higher than any of the period fertility levels over the entire 35-year period. The reason for this is the so-called tempo effect, which depresses P-TFRs as long as the mean age of childbearing is increasing.

Age-specific fertility rates for period and cohorts

	1980–1985	1985–1990	1990–1995	1995–2000	2000–2005	2005–2010	2010–2015
45–49	0	0	0	0	0	0	1
40–44	4	4	4	4	5	7	9
35–39	19	19	22	24	29	37	46
30–34	52	53	61	65	74	85	93
25–29	101	99	105	99	95	89	88
20–24	112	93	85	71	59	51	44
15–19	30	21	20	15	13	11	8
P-TFR	1.60	1.45	1.48	1.39	1.38	1.40	1.45
C-TFR	*1.65 for those who were 15–19 in 1980–85*						

Empirically observed birth statistics tend to be given by age and calendar years. If we want to know how many children a cohort of women had on average over their life course we would have to wait until the cohort under consideration has had their last children, which may be (with some rare exceptions) age 45. Since, in most countries, women have most of the children in their 20s and 30s this means that one could only get information on the "quantum" of fertility, i.e. the average number of children born per woman around two decades after the time when most of the children were born. For this reason, most of the fertility indicators used are period indicators in the sense that they measure the intensity of childbearing for calendar years.

The Total Fertility Rate (TFR) – see Box 1.1 – has gained particular prominence over the past years as the most frequently used indicator of period fertility. It summarizes the childbearing of a so-called synthetic cohort. It gives the average number of children born to a group of women who would be exposed over their reproductive life span to all the age-specific fertility rates observed in calendar year t for all age groups. In the Lexis diagram this refers to the vertical block above the points A–C. Unlike a real cohort of women (which goes along the diagonal) this synthetic cohort does not reflect the reproductive behavior of any real group of women but of a hypothetical cohort of women who, over their life course, experience the birth intensities at every age that is observed for year t.

This TFR is widely used as a measure of the level of fertility that is adjusted for the distorting influence of age structures, since it is based on age-specific rates and gives every age-group equal weight. It is, however, rather sensitive to so-called tempo distortions resulting from the postponement of childbearing, as is currently the case in many countries. The phenomenon is explained in Box 1.1. If these tempo distortions are not taken into account, misleading policy messages can be derived from this indicator (Sobotka & Lutz, 2010). But there are good ways to adjust for this distortion through the calculation of tempo-adjusted TFRs (VID & IIASA, 2020).

Multi-dimensional population dynamics

The age pyramid is one of the most frequently used and most informative demographic charts. As shown in Figure 1.3, it stratifies the population by age groups (in this case 5-year age groups) with women given on the right and men on the left and the youngest age groups at the bottom and the oldest at the top. In the case of a young population the pyramid is broader at the base, reflecting the fact that there are more children than people at higher ages. If the population is stratified by a further demographic characteristic, such as the level of education (as shown in Figure 1.3 by different shadings) then the bar representing each age-group of men and women can be further sub-divided into these categories. Comparing different pyramids for different populations or different points in time for the same population can give a useful summary picture of the salient demographic features and their changes.

The comparison of two age pyramids at subsequent points in time (such as 2000 and 2005 in the case of Figure 1.3) can also help to explain the principle of cohort component projections – which is the dominant form of doing population projections – including its multi-dimensional generalization. While this method is usually explained in terms of matrix notion (the reader can find this in any standard demographic methods textbook), here we will introduce it intuitively by way of describing the relationships between the two pyramids. The dominant feature of this model of population dynamics is that, over five years, the pyramid with 5-year age groups is moved one step up. Everybody gets five years older over five years of time. However, some people do not survive these five years and thus drop out. This is covered by a set of age- and sex-specific mortality rates (which in the case considered here are also education-specific). The standard way of measuring mortality in demography and summarizing it in terms of life expectancies is the key demographic model of a life table, which is explained in Box 1.2.

Box 1.2   Definition of a life table

A life table contains several columns with the following notation:

A life table

Column	Notation	
1	$(x, x+n)$	Age interval between two exact ages stated in years
2	$_nq_x$	Probability of dying between ages x and x+n
3	l_x	Number left alive at age x, starting from a radix of 100,000 at birth
4	$_nd_x$	Number of life table deaths in the age interval x to x+n
5	$_nL_x$	Person years lived in the interval x to x+n
6	T_x	Total person years lived above age x
7	e_x^0	Average number of years of life remaining at age x

Empirically, a life table is entered through a set of observed age-specific mortality rates for a given period and these are converted into age-specific probabilities of dying.

Example   Abridged life table for the total United States population, 1997

(1) (x to x + n)	(2) $_nq_x$	(3) l_x	(4) $_nd_x$	(5) $_nL_x$	(6) T_x	(7) e_x^0
< 1	0.00723	100,000	723	99,371	7,650,789	76.5
1–4	0.00144	99,277	143	396,774	7,551,418	76.1
5–9	0.00092	99,135	91	495,432	7,154,644	72.2
10–14	0.00116	99,043	115	494,997	6,659,212	67.2
15–19	0.00374	98,929	370	493,801	6,164,215	62.3
20–24	0.00492	98,558	485	491,596	5,670,414	57.5
25–29	0.00509	98,073	499	489,137	5,178,818	52.8
30–34	0.00630	97,574	615	486,397	4,689,680	48.1
35–39	0.00840	96,959	814	482,862	4,203,284	43.4
40–44	0.01196	96,145	1149	478,017	3,720,422	38.7
45–49	0.01757	94,996	1669	471,055	3,242,404	34.1
50–54	0.02618	93,327	2443	460,915	2,771,349	29.7
55–59	0.04123	90,884	3747	445,708	2,310,434	25.4
60–64	0.06457	87,136	5627	422,450	1,864,727	21.4
65–69	0.09512	81,510	7753	389,159	1,442,277	17.7
70–74	0.14365	73,757	10595	343,402	1,053,118	14.3
75–79	0.20797	63,162	13135	284,018	709,716	11.2
80–84	0.31593	50,026	15805	211,466	425,698	8.5
85–89	0.46155	34,221	15795	130,736	214,232	6.3
90–94	0.62682	18,427	11550	60,800	83,496	4.5
95–99	0.77325	6876	5317	18,825	22,696	3.3
100+	1.0000	1559	1559	3871	3871	2.5

Source: NCHS; National Vital Statistics Reports Vol. 47, No. 19.

The youngest age group in the shifted pyramid is then filled with the babies born over the period resulting from applying age- and education-specific fertility rates to the respective groups of women and adjusting for child mortality. In addition to survival, the shape of the age pyramid, while shifted one step up, can also change through migration. Over the five-year interval, people of different sex, age and education levels can enter the population under consideration or leave it. This is captured in the model through sets of age-, sex- and education-specific in- and out-migration rates. And in the case of populations stratified by level of education there is a third way in which the shifted age pyramid can differ from the original one, and this is through people who move over the 5-year period from a lower to a higher education category. Since, in most countries, such education transitions happen at younger ages after reaching young adulthood, the educational attainment distributions within each cohort tend to be very stable. This stability along cohort lines is an important feature that allows us to project educational attainment distributions for several decades into the future as well as for reconstructing populations by level of education for the past decades. This will be discussed and illustrated in more detail in Chapter 2.

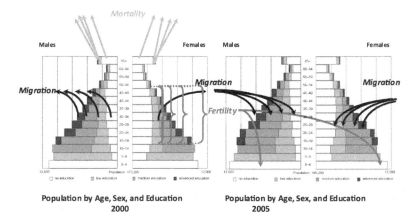

Population by Age, Sex, and Education
2000

Population by Age, Sex, and Education
2005

Figure 1.3   Age and education pyramids for a hypothetical country at two points in time, indicating the principle of multi-dimensional cohort component population projections

To summarize again this basic procedure of modeling population dynamics and forecasting the population by age, sex and level of education in 5-year steps: essentially, the whole pyramid is shifted up by one 5-year step with people staying in their respective sex and education groups but becoming five years older. But the shifted age pyramid above age 5 is not identical to the original one above age 0 because some people die (which is covered by assumed age-, sex- and education-specific mortality rates) and some people enter and leave the population over the 5-year period. In addition, in the younger age groups some people can move from lower to higher educational attainment categories. Finally, the youngest age group in the projected pyramid is filled through babies born over the five years, as calculated by applying age-specific fertility rates to the female population and adjusting the number of births for child mortality.

If population dynamics is addressed with a model that only considers the age- and sex-structure of populations then the only three forces to be captured are fertility, mortality, and migration. If the educational attainment structure is also considered as a third demographic dimension, then one also has to account for education transitions as well as for education differentials in fertility, mortality and migration. As the different projections and scenarios discussed in the following chapters will show, differences in future fertility patterns have by far the biggest influence on long-term population trends because of the multiplier effect: the more children born will result, in due course, in many more grandchildren, and so on. And given the strong differences in fertility levels of women with different levels of education – in many African countries women without formal education have, on average, about three times more children than women with completed secondary education – improvements in female education become one of the key determinants in future global population dynamics.

Demographic data on global human capital

Sources of demographic data

Demography is widely considered to be a primarily data-driven science. In the spectrum of social sciences ranging from entirely qualitative to very quantitative statistical approaches it is clearly positioned at the quantitative end. This is consistent with one of its previously stated definitions, as the mathematics of groups of people. Mathematical models together with theories serve the purpose of putting data into a context, making sense of patterns appearing in the data, analyzing and interpreting observed empirical trends, and drawing up some conclusions and assumptions for projections. Hence, first and foremost, demography is an empirical discipline and demographic data are its cornerstones.

Demographic data are, in the first instance, counts of people in different places or with different characteristics. Such counts have long been considered as useful by political leaders for military, economic and other planning purposes. There are records of early counts in ancient Babylonian, Egyptian and Chinese cultures. The Biblical books report that Moses, who may have lived in the 13th century BCE, conducted two censuses (Exodus 30: 12, 38: 25–26; Numbers 1: 2, 26: 2). The Romans made census taking – actually, *census* is a Latin word derived from *censio* meaning assessing – part of a regular assessment of the number of households for taxation and military purposes. In Christian tradition, the best-known example of such a census is described in Luke 2: 1–3, a text read in virtually every Christmas service: "In those days Caesar Augustus issued a decree that a census should be taken of the entire Roman world." But counts of households and heads have been part of many cultures and religions. It is reported that one of the first things the Prophet Mohammed did after having moved with his followers from Mecca to Medina was to take a census of the population of the city. Another prominent census is the so-called Domesday Book, in which William the Conqueror, in 1086 – twenty years after having conquered the country – had a count of all houses in England. Many of these early counts were more interested in the number of households (often defined as hearths) than in the number of people living in them. A 1427 census (*catasto*) in Florence was probably one of the first to actually assess all individuals living in the households (Weeks, 2014). The 1703 census of Iceland was the first comprehensive census of an entire country providing not only the head count but also structures by age, sex, place of residence and socio-economic status. It thus started the era of modern censuses which aim at complete counts of the entire resident populations of countries, collecting information on selected individual characteristics that are considered relevant.

While censuses provide information on population size and structures at a given point in time, they do not give direct information on the processes by which populations change, in particular births, deaths and migratory movements. Data collection on these demographic changes followed a different historical evolution, mostly in the context of religious record keeping, or parish books in the Christian tradition. From the 15th century on, such parish records have been kept in Italy and France, and the fragments of them that were maintained still serve as an important source of historical demography. In the 16th century, church authorities in the context of the protestant reformation and counter-reformation encouraged parish priests to take more systematically such records of all baptisms, marriages and funerals, but the practice seems to have spread very slowly, and hardly any comprehensive data were collected centrally. Such central collection by church authorities, partly in collaboration with state authorities, only started in the 18th century in the Nordic countries. In Sweden, in 1749, a central system of population statistics (*Tabellverket*) was introduced in which church registers were organized in such a way that they maintained information on the number of residents and some of their characteristics as well as complete records of births, deaths, marriages and movements into and out of the parishes. This allowed for systematic annual calculations of demographic rates, with both the numerators (vital events) and denominators (resident population at risk of experiencing these events) available. For the territory of Finland, which was until 1809 part of the Swedish kingdom, such series of annual birth, death and marriage rates could even be reconstructed back to 1722. This makes the Finnish time series, which will be presented in more detail in the following section on demographic transition, the world's longest annual demographic time series. This combination of statistical information on population counts and changes over time (assessed yearly or monthly) have developed further into modern population registers, which exist in all Nordic countries as well as the Netherlands and an increasing number of European countries. Such comprehensive and computerized population registers are, in a way, the ideal source of demographic data because both the numerators and denominators can be derived simultaneously even when sub-divided by certain demographic characteristics. For example, while the calculation of adult mortality rates by level of education still presents a major problem in many countries (numerators and denominators come from different sources and deceased people cannot be asked in surveys about their education) population registers can instantly provide any such data.

In most countries of the world however, the statistical traditions of census taking and of vital registration have developed independently and are conducted by different branches of government. While censuses are mostly organized centrally by national statistical authorities and, in the case of developing countries, often with support from international organizations, the collection of data on births and deaths is typically done by local authorities in the municipalities and their registry offices. In most industrialized countries these decentralized systems of vital registry function fairly well and produce comprehensive counts of all births and deaths – although often with some time lags. In many developing countries the systems of vital registration are less reliable and often incomplete. Hence, for many developing countries the series of censuses which are typically carried out every ten years according to standardized forms and often with international technical support are the most reliable sources of comprehensive demographic information, i.e. data collected for the entire population of a country. Since censuses often also include questions about how many children a woman has had and how many of them survived up to the time of the census, and where they lived 5 or 10 years before the census, such census data are often also used to indirectly estimate levels of fertility, child mortality and migration.

Given the unsatisfactory situation for comprehensive vital statistics in many countries and the fact that the number of characteristics (demographic dimensions) included in such data sets is very limited, even in countries with well-developed systems, sample surveys have tried to fill this gap in getting more detailed information on demographic characteristics. In addition to surveys carried out at the national level, there have been also big and coordinated demographic data collection efforts at the international level. Starting with the World Fertility Survey (WFS) in the 1980s and later through many rounds of Demographic and Health Surveys (DHS), a huge amount of individual level data was collected via so far over 400 surveys in 90 countries of the world, primarily on topics of fertility and contraception as well as child health and other aspects of family health. For many of these countries the DHS-based information presents the best available data on fertility, child mortality and health and associated factors. Since sample sizes tend to be big enough in most cases, these representative surveys can provide reliable demographic information on these variables. The situation is more difficult with respect to estimates of adult mortality and migration patterns. For internal as well as international migration, such surveys cannot provide much information because they typically do not include questions on migration histories, and the sample sizes are too small for a truly comprehensive assessment of movements. For the estimation of adult mortality, the problem is that deceased people cannot be asked anymore and asking other family members only works well in the case of child mortality reported by mothers. For this reason, many estimates of adult mortality and life expectancy, as published in international databases, are actually derived from model life tables for which the level of child mortality is the only reliable empirical input.

Another more recent approach to compensate for the lack of comprehensive vital statistics and other health-related information in many developing countries has been in the form of the so-called Demographic Surveillance Systems (DSS). These are regular surveys in certain well-defined smaller areas in selected urban or rural sites in which – at intervals of a few months – specifically trained field staff visit all households to register any changes in terms of births and deaths and other relevant aspects since the last visit, thus providing unique longitudinal information. Most of these DSS sites collaborate in the context of the INDEPTH Network, in which they share their data and thus provide the necessary evidence to influence health and social policies in their countries and internationally. So far, they cover over 4 million people who live in the 53 populations covered by surveillance systems run by 46 research centers in 20 countries in Africa, Asia and Oceania.

There are also several internationally standardized demographic surveys in high income countries that collect more detailed demographic, health and socio-economic information than is provided by the comprehensive systems of vital registration and censuses. In the field of fertility, these are the Family and Fertility Surveys (FFS) and the Gender and Generation Surveys (GGS) in many European countries. The Survey of Health, Ageing and Retirement in Europe (SHARE) is the largest panel study in Europe and has a specific focus on people aged 50 and older. Since 2004 it has conducted 380,000 in-depth interviews in 28 European countries and Israel with, at the time of writing, up to eight waves. The truly longitudinal nature of these micro data has the great advantage that changes over time can be observed for the same individuals, which offers more possibilities for studying causality as compared with only comparing cross-sectional surveys at different points in time, where the individuals interviewed are different in each round. This data are similar in nature, with some national longitudinal studies such as the US Health and Retirement Study (HRS) and the English Longitudinal Study of Ageing (ELSA). There are many other international surveys which also include pieces of demographic information, such as the European Labor Force Survey or European and global health surveys.

The traditional demographic data collected through censuses and vital registration, and the more recent data collected through surveys, complete population registers, and Demographic Surveillance Systems have been further complemented by data derived from remote sensing and, more recently, from telecommunications/social media. Remote sensing in the form of aerial photography and satellite imagery has for decades been used to study changes in land-use, including settlement patterns. While such images cannot directly provide demographic data, they do give information on the number and even size of houses, and can thus be used for rough estimates of changing population sizes based on assumptions of average household sizes. They cannot, however, provide information on the composition of the population by age, sex, or level of education, even though the size of the house and its neighborhood may give some indication about the wealth of the household. Much more information about the demographic, social and economic characteristics of individual people can potentially be derived from so-called big data. In particular, social media or internet search engines have recently been used to estimate migration patterns or even short-term changes in pregnancy rates depending on the topics searched for on the internet. However, with many of these new data it is not clear how representative they are for the entire population because the use of these specific media is neither complete nor randomly distributed. Another use of big data that still seems to be in its very early stage is derived from new high-tech approaches related to face recognition on surveillance cameras, and other approaches of identification of individuals, combined with machine learning and artificial intelligence.

It is not yet clear what new ways of collecting demographic data will develop in the future as technology progresses further. What is clear, however, is that most of these new technologies pose great challenges in terms of data protection and privacy. Here, the development of legal standards to protect basic personality rights must keep pace with the introduction of new technologies collecting information from an increasing number of life domains. There has always been some tension between the competing objectives of collecting comprehensive information for necessary demographic analyses and protecting the privacy of individual citizens. A famous example is the controversy around the West German census originally planned for 1981, then postponed to 1983 when it was canceled due to massive protests. It was conducted in much reduced form in 1987. The next full census was then only held in 2011 for the united Germany. One of the lessons learned from this is that in order to collect reliable demographic information there must be a minimal level of trust amongst the population that the data will be used to their advantage rather than against them. In addition, the information collected for all residents in a compulsory way – participation in censuses is compulsory in most countries – should be parsimonious and restricted to the essentials. For more detailed information, sample surveys in which the anonymity of the respondent is assured are the more appropriate tool. Censuses, however, are still needed for the foreseeable future in order to provide information about the total count of people and their basic demographic structures, which is a prerequisite for drawing representative samples.

Data on world population and human capital 1950–2100

In this section, after having briefly summarized the sources of demographic data and how they are derived from different systems of data collection, I will briefly describe how best to get access to harmonized data for all countries in the world. The focus here will be exclusively on international databases since, for national level data, access to information depends greatly on specific national conditions. Hence, if the reader is interested in demographic data for one specific country it is best to look both for data provided by national statistical agencies as well as the internationally comparable data provided by the international databases described in the following.

For many decades the United Nations Population Division (UNPD), which is part of the United Nations Department of Social and Economic Affairs (DESA) at the United Nations headquarters in New York, had the central collection and harmonization of consistent demographic data for all countries in the world as one of its main tasks. It is important to emphasize the harmonization and consistency aspect because, unlike the data collected and published by the United Nations Statistics Division from national statistical offices around the world in sometimes inconsistent ways as provided directly by the various countries, the Population

Division further processes the data in order to produce internally consistent data for standardized time intervals and age groups for all countries. These standardized data start in 1950 and present population sizes and age structures for men and women in five-year intervals and for five-year age groups and selected derived indicators, such as age-dependency ratios, i.e. the relative sizes of certain broader age groups at specific points in time. For users interested in single years of time, interpolations to single years are also given. In terms of population change, the database also provides fertility, mortality and migration rates over five-year intervals as well as population growth rates. All these estimates from 1950 onwards are updated at intervals of two to three years and can be accessed at https://population.un.org/wpp/.

This United Nations database also provides population projections for all countries up to 2100. This is why the database is also called "World Population Prospects". As will be discussed in detail in Chapter 4 on demographic futures, the UNPD currently offers the user three variants as well as the results of a probabilistic population projection model. The medium variant is by far the most frequently used scenario and can also be interpreted as the trajectory that is considered most likely from today's perspective. The high and low variants are based on alternative assumptions which, for each country, assume a Total Fertility Rate that is 0.5 children higher and lower than the medium assumption, while mortality and migration assumptions are identical. The medium variant of the World Population Prospects 2019 assessment gives a projection under which the world population will reach 8.55 billion in 2030, 9.74 billion in 2050 and 10.88 billion in 2100. As will be discussed in Chapter 4 these long-term projections greatly depend on the speed of future fertility decline in Africa, the "ultimate" fertility levels to be reached in low fertility countries and the potentials for future increases in life expectancy.

In the context of the focus on multi-dimensional demography chosen by this Advanced Introduction, it is important to note that the above-described UN database only considers the population of each country stratified by age and sex and does not address further important sources of population heterogeneity. This has been the conventional approach in demography until recently and is still reflected in databases and published population projections of most statistical offices around the world. Based on the widely acknowledged evidence that educational attainment is a key source of relevant population heterogeneity in addition to age and sex (Lutz &

KC, 2011), the Wittgenstein Centre for Demography and Global Human Capital (WIC) – which is a collaboration of the International Institute for Applied Systems Analysis (IIASA), the Vienna Institute of Demography (VID) of the Austrian Academy of Sciences, and the Department of Demography of the University of Vienna – has produced a harmonized and consistent database for demographic indicators of all countries from 1950 to 2100. It is comparable to that of the UN, with the difference that indicators are also stratified by four to eight different levels of educational attainment (the user can choose the level of detail) in addition to age and sex. This database can be accessed under the Wittgenstein Centre Human Capital Data Explorer (http://www.wittgensteincentre.org/dataexplorer).

The Wittgenstein Centre currently updates its database every five years. The latest 2018 update was published together with the Joint Research Centres (JRC) of the European Commission (Lutz et al., 2018). The database is accessible from the link given above and consists of a data explorer, which results in tabular output, and a graphic explorer, which plots age pyramids by level of education (superimposed by color to the usual age and sex distribution given by the pyramid). Figure 1.4 shows the two global age and education pyramids for 1950 and 2020 as provided by the WIC graphic explorer. Similar pyramids can be derived for every country and every point in time (in 5-year steps) and for up to 2100 under a number of different future scenarios. In addition, line charts can be derived which plot the size of respective education groups over time without showing the age and sex

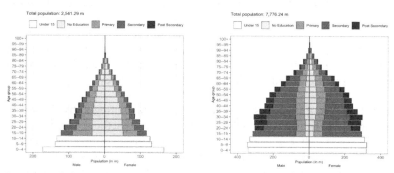

Source: WIC Graphic Explorer.

Figure 1.4   Age and education pyramids for the world population in 1950 (left) and 2020 (right)

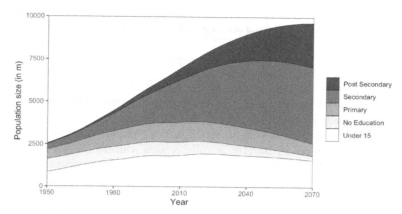

Source: WIC Graphic Explorer.

Figure 1.5   World population (in million) by level of highest
educational attainment as observed/reconstructed for
1950–2020 and projected under the middle-of-the-road
SSP2 scenario 2020–2070

detail. Such a figure for the world population, under the middle of the road
SSP2 scenario (the scenarios will be explained in more detail in Chapter 4),
is given in Figure 1.5. The figures clearly show that among the entire world
population aged 15 and above, more than one third had never had the opportunity to visit school in 1950 and less than a quarter had some secondary or
higher education. Today, the vast majority of the world adult population has
at least some secondary education, and post-secondary education is rapidly
increasing among the younger cohorts.

The WIC data explorer also provides data for all countries and all points in
time in tabular form for a large number of population and human capital
stock variables (such as population sizes and educational attainment distribution as well as gender gaps in education) as well as flow variables. These flow
variables include all the standard demographic rates as they are listed by the
UN with additional differentiation by level of education for many of them.

For those readers interested in still more detailed information about demographic flow variables in the field of fertility, mortality and migration, there
are specific specialized databases. However, these do not cover all countries

in the world, but only those for which high quality data are available. In the following I will briefly highlight the human fertility and human mortality databases as well as a database offering estimates on global bilateral migration flows.

The Human Mortality Data Base is organized by a collaboration of the Max Planck Institute for Demographic Research (MPIDR) and the Demography Department of the University of Berkeley. It provides very detailed and internationally comparable mortality and population data for currently 41 countries (see https://www.mortality.org/). The Human Fertility Data Base (HFD) is organized by MPIDR in collaboration with the Vienna Institute of Demography of the Austrian Academy of Sciences and consists of two segments: https://www.humanfertility.org/ gives the highest quality data that could be collected for 32 countries, and the Human Fertility Collection (https://www.fertilitydata.org) supplementing the HFD by incorporating a variety of valuable fertility data from diverse, not necessarily official, data sources. As for internationally comparable migration data, the situation is more complex because these data are not directly measured by national or international statistical agencies and can only be estimated indirectly. One such comprehensive estimate of global bilateral migration flows for five-year intervals between 1990 and 2010 is available at http://www.global-migration .info, with a recent update given at https://www.nature.com/articles/s41597 -019-0089-3. Internationally comparable demographic data are also available from the Population Reference Bureau (https://www.prb.org/) which regularly publishes World Population Data Sheets.

With this, admittedly not exhaustive, list of important international databases with comparable demographic data for many countries around the world, the reader will be in the position to extract abundant information on past and possible future trends in any country of choice. Together with the basic demographic concepts sketched in the first part of the chapter this offers the first basis for empirical demographic analyses. However, since data without theories are blind, the data alone do not tell us what to make of the data and how to interpret them, we need to next turn to the discussion of demographic theories. Unlike in most other introductions to demography or textbooks on demographic methods, here we put a heavy emphasis on demographic theory and offer the first glimpse of a possible new unified demographic theory. This consists of three established demographic theories.

present but also forecast decades into the future, based on robust models. Unlike most other social sciences, demographic models and theories can forecast some of the most fundamental social changes decades into the future in a quantitative way.

The Unified Demographic Theory introduced here is based on a multi-dimensional approach and has three constituent demographic theories which are closely linked to each other. First, the theory of demographic metabolism (DM) will be introduced and discussed with regard to its applications in the following section. It is so powerful as a predictive tool that it can help to anticipate future trends not only in the usual demographic variables but also in other highly relevant fields such as values, national identities and deeply engrained behavioral patterns – if these characteristics and patterns are established in young adulthood and then essentially maintained unchanged through the rest of the life course. If these conditions are met, social changes in a broad array of topics can be anticipated for decades into the future through the process of intergenerational replacement, which was termed by Ryder (1965) "demographic metabolism". Since this approach of cohort-specific analysis implicitly or explicitly lies at the basis of all modeling of demographic changes it will be described first.

The theory of demographic transition (DT) is the oldest and most prominent of the three demographic theories and essentially says that a fertility transition based on conscious family limitation follows a mortality decline (with a varying time lag) and that, once started, it will continue reaching virtually all segments of a given population resulting in fertility around or below replacement and that this is an irreversible process. All existing long-term population projections are, in one way or another, based on this theory of demographic transition.

The notion of a demographic dividend (DD) is the youngest of the three theories and was originally coined to describe the economic benefits derived by a population that goes through demographic transition and, as a consequence, experiences a decline in the proportion of the population at young ages and an increase in the working age population (Bloom et al., 2003). Unified Growth Theory (Galor, 2011) in economics identifies demographic transition as the root cause of the modern economic rise. A more recent framing of the concept of the demographic dividend in the context of multi-dimensional demography highlights the importance of improving educational composition of the population for economic growth and multiple other benefits. Among other things this demographic theory can well explain the rise of the Asian Tigers and the even more consequential rise of China, which fundamentally changes the global geopolitical landscape. As will be explained in subsequent sections, this theory of demographic dividend is not only powerful in explaining past economic growth but it has predictive power in forecasting economic development and other increases in human well-being, including the resilience to environmental change.

The combination of these three demographic theories described here presents a powerful approach to understanding some of the most consequential changes in human history and helps to anticipate future equally important changes. In this respect, these theories may even be superior to the leading sociological and economic theories. The problem is that most people – including most demographers – are not aware of this great potential because they have not thought about it in this way. This is why this Advanced Introduction puts a strong emphasis on theory.

What is a theory in demography?

Part of the confusion and debate around the role of theories in demography has to do with different views of what a theory is. The *Cambridge Dictionary* describes the usage of theory both in science as well as in public usage, in its most general form, as "a formal statement of the rules on which a subject of study is based or of ideas that are suggested to explain a fact or event or, more generally, an opinion or explanation" (*Cambridge Dictionary*, 2020). While this definition is so general that almost everybody can agree with it, it is also not very helpful in distinguishing a well-founded scientific theory from just an informed opinion or a certain more or less arbitrarily chosen model.

While there is no space here for an extensive theory of science considerations, it suffices to say that the philosophy-of-science approach chosen here will follow Karl Popper, whose methodology holds that scientific theories are characterized by being able to provide predictions that future observations might reveal to be false (Popper, 1959). This approach has become dominant in modern science and, in particular, in the natural sciences. It tries to distinguish between scientific theories and other theories (called pseudo-theories) that seem to be able to explain almost everything but cannot be falsified. It was in particular the work by Marx, Freud and Adler at the time that seemed to be able to provide an answer and an explanation to almost every experience or observation, which they called theory but which was not able to come up with testable predictions. Because such theories that give the impression of being able to explain everything – any fact can be interpreted as supporting them in one way or another (something called confirmation bias) – cannot possibly be falsified, they are not considered scientific theories by Popper.[1] In other words, a key constituent of a scientific theory is its testability. And in order to be testable any theory must have predictive power.

In the broader field of social sciences, the word "theory" is often used not only in terms of its predictive power but also for its explanatory and descriptive power, where phenomena that are already known are retro-spectively explained by a given theory. Few of such theories also allow a prospective test of the proposed theoretical understanding. Hence, under the strong definition of predictive power described above, such explanatory patterns would not qualify for being called scientific theories when they focus on description and explanation rather than prediction (Lakatos, 1978; Popper, personal communication, see Note 1; Wright, 1971). In the natural sciences this testing can usually be done by carrying out experiments. In social sciences, where large scale experiments are difficult or impossible to conduct (although there are some "natural experiments"), predictions of the evolution of social phenomena usually require some quantification of the phenomenon that shall be explained. While this is easy in quantitative disciplines such as demography as well as in many fields of economics it is much more difficult in the qualitative social sciences and the humanities.

What does predictive power mean in demography? Here it is important to distinguish between theories dealing with predicting individual behavior or specific components of change such as fertility and migration and those predicting aggregate level changes in terms of population size and structures. Given the definition of demography as studying the chang-ing size and structures, the adjective "demographic" in the strict sense should only be applied to theories trying to predict such aggregate level changes of the population. In addition, there is a multitude of theories relating to individual behavior, such as reproductive behavior resulting in different fertility levels, individual choices with respect to migration, or health-related behavior resulting in different mortality patterns that matter for the determinants of demographic change and thus indirectly and partially affect aggregate demographic change. In this sense, theories trying to predict fertility, mortality or migration can only be seen as *partially demographic theories*, because they only address specific components of overall changes in population size and structures. We will discuss these relevant theories in the following chapters, which describe these components of change, but we will not consider them "demographic theories" in the strict sense.

Demography as an "intervention science"

The question of explanatory versus predictive power of the social sciences is not an academic ivory tower discussion but is directly linked to the visibility and acceptance of the humanities and social sciences (HSS) in society and, as a partial consequence of this, in the funding that society provides for different scientific disciplines. It was recently suggested that the HSS should try to find attractive broader paradigms that can help to serve the dual purpose of setting priorities within given disciplinary research traditions and also communicate the value of such research to the public. These new paradigms or narratives about what the social sciences can do that is of direct relevance to society should effectively help focus research on the essential questions of the 21st century. In this context, Lutz (2012, 2015) proposed to distinguish between two very different approaches in the HSS labeled "Identity Sciences" and "Intervention Sciences". They differ in their objectives in trying to better understand (a) who we are and (b) how we can manage our future. In the end, this goes back to the three classic questions of philosophy: who am I, where do I come from, and where am I going? A fourth question should be added today: how can I change the world around me in order to have a better life? These questions not only apply to every individual, but also to groups of people as well as entire societies. The first two questions are addressed by what has occasionally and appropriately been labeled "Identity Sciences", which include most of the humanities and qualitative social sciences. It is a basic psychological fact that every human being and every functioning group of people need identities (Maslow, 1954). The better we understand these identities in their historical and cultural contexts, the better is our knowledge basis for organizing our lives as individuals and as groups. Since most people care to know where they come from, this function of the HSS cannot be appreciated enough.

To give an answer to the other two questions and to understand where we are going and how to change the world around us in order to have a better life, we need another function of the social sciences. At the individual level, we need models of human behavior (typically situated in physiology and psychology) and, at the societal level, we need theories of socio-economic change with predictive power (Lutz, 2013). The natural sciences are equipped with many such theories that make it possible to come up with conditional predictions, providing the scientific basis to intervene in the course of events, whether this means curing a previously deadly disease, traveling to the moon or changing the energy mix in order to reduce greenhouse gas emissions. But these theories are often not able to deal with the complex dynamics within social systems. Wherever there are groups of human beings, the social sciences are needed to help understand the complex interactions among people. In this sense and with a view to the future, the social sciences also have a comparable function to the natural sciences, namely to better understand the basic mechanisms through which our societies work and change (which is the task of basic research) and, based on this knowledge, to identify and evaluate possible alternative interventions. To make sure that these are meaningful, we have to understand which forces can be influenced and which cannot, and what are the likely consequences of no intervention as compared with various possible interventions. The consequences of such alternative possible interventions can be described in the form of alternative scenarios. To account for this particular aspect of the social sciences, they can labeled as "Intervention Sciences" (Lutz, 2012). This notion was inspired by the change of name of the Oxford Department of Social Policy to "Social Policy and Intervention" which now defines itself as "a multidisciplinary centre of excellence for research and teaching in social policy, and in the development and systematic evaluation of social interventions and policies" (University of Oxford, 2020).

Can there be true predictive power in the social sciences? With economics being considered as part of the HSS, prediction is precisely what most economic models try to do, although with mixed success and for relatively short time horizons. Even when the behavior of people as individuals or as groups is considered to be less deterministic than most of the forces studied in the natural sciences, there is no reason not to try to come up with similar models of social change in which the consequences of certain interventions on future outcomes are predicted within specified uncertainty ranges. There is a whole body of literature on predictive power in probabilistic terms which cannot be reviewed here (see Diekmann, 1995).

Later in this volume we will present several examples of scenarios (conditional demographic predictions) and probabilistic projections in the field of population forecasting. They show, for instance, for several decades into the future, how different interventions in the form of alternative education expansion scenarios result not only in different educational attainment distributions, but also in different total population sizes and levels of child mortality, since fertility and child mortality vary in consistent and predictable ways with the level of mothers' education. They can also help to anticipate the future adaptive capacity to climate change under different education scenarios (Lutz, Muttarak, et al., 2014; Lutz & Muttarak, 2017).

In times of accelerating social change around the world, such intervention science that identifies and models the systematic and predictable elements of social change is more needed than ever before. Societies that want to actively shape their future rather than to just leave it to be determined by outside forces or simply the random processes of history crucially need such intervention sciences. Social scientists should be given the right incentives to enter this high-risk but also high-potential-impact field of science. However, apart from economists, not many social scientists dare to move beyond the presumably safe field of the analysis of past data and use their models to address the likely longer-term consequences of alternative interventions in the near future. Strengthened and emancipated by emphasizing their role as evidence- and theory-based intervention sciences, the social sciences may more successfully make their contribution and be recognized as an equal partner with the natural sciences in jointly addressing the big questions of our common human future. And demography can be a leader in this enterprise.

"Functional causality" in intervention sciences: the effect of education[2]

A key concern in the social sciences in general and in predictive models in particular is the question of causality. Conditional predictions are only credible if the assumed underlying mechanisms, on the basis of which the consequences of alternative interventions are assessed, are true, i.e. causal in nature. One always has to be aware of the possibility that the assumed

demography until it was combined with the powerful analytical tools of multi-dimensional (multi-state) demography in recent years. These multi-dimensional methods, which were originally developed in the 1970s, facilitated its operationalization and the calculation of actual forecasts based on demographic metabolism (Lutz, 2013). In an article entitled "Demographic Metabolism: A Predictive Theory of Socioeconomic Change", I tried to present a consistent theoretical framework that enlarged Ryder's original framework by including both intra-cohort transitions and inter-cohort changes in the model. It was also put to work in terms of producing actual numerical projections of the changing composition of populations that are sub-divided according to clearly defined, observable sources of heterogeneity or demographic dimensions. Its most prominent application was to the reconstruction and projection of the changing composition of populations by age, sex and different levels of educational attainment for all countries in the world (Lutz, Butz, et al., 2014; Lutz & KC, 2011), and it has also been used for projecting other demographic and non-demographic characteristics, as will be discussed below.

In the following I will describe the historical origins of the theory, define its conceptual elements in terms of four propositions and demonstrate the enormous potentials of the demographic metabolism approach for capturing and forecasting social change. Actually, the idea that societies change as new generations "take over" is already found in early writings on this topic by pre-Socratic philosophers and in Confucian philosophy in various expressions. It is indeed surprising that such a plausible concept, which reflects shared experiences in most families, companies and institutions across all cultures and times, has not received systematic and formalized scientific attention as a key driving force of social change. The principle of inter-cohort change has neither been applied to the systematic analysis of historical evolutions nor been used as the basis for forecasting.

In more recent history, the thought that comes closest to the idea of viewing social change as being driven by the succession of generations, can be found in the writings of art historians in the late 19th and early 20th centuries who explain the change in artistic styles and techniques as being a consequence of the replacement of older generations of artists by new ones (Dilthey, 1900). The first social scientist to offer a comprehensive synthesis of this view of history was Karl Mannheim. In his essay on

"The Problem of Generations" (first published in German in 1928 and translated into English in 1952), Mannheim contrasts the "romantic" views of art history with the "biological" perspective (Mannheim, 1952, p. 278) which can be interpreted as demographic.

More than a generation after Mannheim, the Canadian-American demographer Norman Ryder coined the notion of "demographic metabolism", which he defines as the "massive process of personnel replacement" driven by the births, lives and deaths of individuals (Ryder, 1965, p. 843). While he saw the flexibility for individuals to change over their lifetime as limited, the appearance of new individuals in the social process provides an opportunity for social transformation. He also made the strong statement that, "The society whose members were immortal would resemble a stagnant pond" (Ryder, 1965, p. 844). He stressed that demographic metabolism is not necessarily an approach to describe social progress but, more neutrally, social change that may go in any direction.

Ryder in this paper also provided the standard definition of a cohort as was already explained in Chapter 1 above. One decisive step in which Lutz (2013) went beyond Ryder was to relax the assumption of strong cohort determinism. The tools of multi-dimensional population dynamics also allow for changes to happen over the life course of cohorts. Hence, the possibility of lifelong learning and changes within birth cohorts can in itself present a force of socio-economic change, such that immortality would no longer necessarily result in Ryder's "stagnant pond". The relative strengths of cohort effects compared with age and period effects depends on the specific characteristic studied. In some applications, such as the modeling by highest educational attainment after a certain age, the characteristic is invariant by definition, in other cases (such as the example of European identity, later) this is a matter of empirical analysis of the past and corresponding assumptions for the future.

Basic premises of the theory of demographic metabolism

The theory of demographic metabolism as specified in Lutz (2013) is a macro-level theory that predicts aggregate-level change. It focuses on the changing composition of a population according to certain critical characteristics of individuals. It can be called a "demographic" theory because it rests firmly on the demographic approach and methodology, particularly the multi-dimensional cohort component model (Keyfitz,

1985; e.g. Rogers, 1975). Its application, however, is not limited to demographic questions. It can be used to predict social change with regard to a wide range of different relevant dimensions as long as they are based on characteristics including values, attitudes and skills that are held by people and have some stability over the individual life course. Hence, the theory uses a demographic paradigm, but it is not primarily intended to explain and forecast demographic variables (such as population size, birth and death rates, migration, etc.).

In more formalized language the four basic propositions of the theory can be specified as:

Proposition 1: *People – individual humans – are the primary building blocks of every population or sub-population of interest and the primary agents of social and economic behavior. Hence, they form the basic elements (atoms) of any theory of aggregate-level social and economic change.*

Comment: Under this approach people may be seen as the atoms of society, who act and interact with each other. Further into this analogy, households may be seen as molecules and different parts of our brains involved in decision making as the "sub-atomic" level. But here it seems sufficient to focus on individuals interacting with other individuals.

Proposition 2: *For any population, members can be sub-divided into disjoint groups (states) according to clearly specified and measurable individual characteristics (in addition to age and sex) for any given point in time.*

Comment: The fact that chronological age changes in parallel with chronological time, makes forecasting of cohorts an easy task: over time, people stay in their state and simply become one year older every calendar year, unless they decease or transition to another state. Hence, using this model for forecasting is based on splitting up the population into groups as defined by the particular characteristics of interest in addition to sub-dividing by age and sex.

Proposition 3: *Over any interval of time, members of a sub-population (state) defined by certain characteristics can move to another state (associated with different characteristics), and these individual transitions can be mathematically described by a set of age- and sex-specific transition rates.*

Comment: A transition to another state can either occur inside the system (to another sub-population), or to the absorbing state (death), or to a state outside the system (out-migration). New individuals arriving (through birth or in-migration) will directly be allocated to one of the states within the system. But not all transitions among a given set of states need to be possible. Sometimes, transitions may be only possible in one direction, such as from lower to higher educational categories or from the single to the married state, from which people may move to the divorced or widowed state but cannot move back. This is called a hierarchical system.

Proposition 4: *If any given population consists of sub-groups that are different from each other with respect to relevant characteristics, then a change over time in the relative size of these sub-groups will result in a change in the overall distribution of these characteristics in the population, and hence in social change.*

Comment: This proposition holds for any characteristic that is, in principle, stable over time. The choice of the characteristic that defines sub-populations depends on the research questions asked. In the following this will be illustrated with respect to two very different characteristics: the highest level of educational attainment and European identity, i.e. whether a person says they have a European identity in addition to a national one.

The multi-dimensional cohort-component model

The life table as a basic demographic tool has already been introduced in the previous chapter. The standard life table only distinguishes between two states, being alive and being dead (single decrement life table). Since mortality levels tend to differ substantially by sex, there is a long tradition of calculating life tables separately for men and women.

Aside from this standard differentiation by age and sex, however, conventional demography still typically considers populations as largely homogeneous. For the application of a life table, this includes the assumption that, for example, all men aged 50–54 have the same risk of dying, despite large differentials related to clearly identifiable risk factors, such as smoking, obesity or level of educational attainment (Caselli et al., 2014). In the case of multi-dimensional demographic analysis, this strong assumption is relaxed and mortality rates can be modeled as being different for sub-groups depending on further characteristics. This is

held. This is indeed a confirmation of the predictive power of the model of demographic metabolism, even during turbulent times when most observers would have expected the opposite.

These findings suggest that the relentless forces of cohort replacement, through which younger and (up to the most recent cohorts) more European-minded cohorts gradually take the place of the older, more nationally oriented cohorts, produce significant and predictable changes in the pattern of European identity. Even in the hypothetical case that the youngest cohorts would show a strong decline in European identities and these were also to be stable over the life course, the model would still show some further increase for a while – still driven by the passing away of the older predominantly nationally minded older cohorts – until a peak level is reached and the average would enter a decline. This illustrates that the demographic metabolism model of cohort replacement cannot only predict continued monotonic trends in one direction, it can also anticipate possible reversals in the aggregate level trends long before they are prevalent in the aggregate empirical data based on information that we may have for the youngest cohorts.

This comparison of predicted versus empirically observed trends in soft characteristic such as stated identities leaves us with an important methodological message for forecasting social trends in general: trend extrapolation is a much less reliable approach to anticipating future developments than decomposing the population into cohorts, assessing the stability of patterns along cohort lines, and then modeling the changing composition of the population through the demographic metabolism model.

The theory of demographic transition

"In traditional societies, fertility and mortality are high. In modern societies, fertility and mortality are low. In between, there is demographic transition" (Demeny, 1968). This brief definition used by Paul Demeny in 1968, for the opening of a paper on historical demographic trends in Austria–Hungary, captures in a nutshell the strengths and weaknesses of the concept of demographic transition (in the following, abbreviated as DT). These three short sentences provide a seemingly clear and plausible narrative which has inspired much of demographic writing on the topic. Yet this definition of DT is also ambiguous and imprecise with very little specific information to the degree that makes it difficult to justify its classification as a theory. It sounds more like an observation combined with a definition or classification, but without predictive power.

As soon as one tries to add more specific content in terms of distinct phases of transition or certain thresholds marking the beginning or end of the transition, then one can quickly come up with counterexamples and the concept loses its general validity. This ambiguity has led to a still ongoing debate among demographers as to whether DT should be called a theory or not. In 1959, Hauser and Duncan (1959) called it a "non-theory". In a comprehensive review of the literature on DT, Kirk (1996) starts out by characterizing DT as one of the best-documented generalizations in the social sciences. He chooses to call DT a theory in the title of his review paper but does not offer a discussion as to what should be the criteria for calling it a theory. Instead, he provides a broad ranging survey of different causal explanations that have been offered in the literature as drivers of the mortality and fertility transitions.

While a substantive discussion about the drivers of the mortality and fertility transitions will be given in the Chapter 3 together with a presentation of the concept of "cognition driven demographic transition", in this chapter I will try to come up with as precise as possible a definition of DT and its predictive power that allows us to classify it as a theory. The challenge is to be general enough in this specification to assure universal applicability under rather heterogeneous country-specific conditions while, at the same time, offering a precise formulation that allows for prediction and even possible falsification. Following up and further building on the four propositions specified for the theory of demographic metabolism in the previous sections we can specify three more propositions for the concept of cognition driven DT presented here.

Proposition 5: *Literacy and improved cognitive abilities through education enhance abstract thinking and foresight and reduce unplanned behavior including health and reproduction related behavior.*

Comment: The mechanisms by which education is translated into an increase in abstraction skills and mental abilities have been described above and will be further discussed in Chapter 3. This proposition is introduced here because it relates directly to the mortality and fertility transitions. It can be interpreted as referring to the building of human capital.

Proposition 6: *Individuals empowered through literacy and education can collaborate to advance the frontier of knowledge and technology and improve public health and the quality of institutions in general.*

Comment: This is the first of the propositions that explicitly addresses the interactions among individual agents with consequences that go beyond the effects of changes in proportions addressed in Proposition 4. It can be interpreted as referring to the building of knowledge capital and institutions.

Proposition 7: *Individuals are in their views, values and priorities influenced by other individuals around them, depending on their proximity and attractiveness/social status.*

Comment: This can be interpreted as referring to the diffusion of values and ideational change. The distribution of such values in a population can either be captured by sub-dividing the population into sub-groups with different values or by more qualitative assessments of changing dominant values. The concept of developmental idealism (Thornton, 2005) also falls under this proposition.

Before I explain how these three propositions, together with the previous four, form the basis for understanding DT, we will first have a look at the history of the concept of DT and some empirical trends in order to better understand what phenomenon we are trying to explain.

Historical origins

The basic idea of DT has a long intellectual history in Europe. The English economist/philosopher John Stuart Mill (1806–1873) rejected the Malthusian pessimism about population growth surpassing food supply by stressing that the increase in national wealth can keep pace with population growth. Interestingly, Mill pointed at the decisive role of female empowerment. Mill believed that women do not want as many children as men do and, if they got their way, the birth rate would decline. He even concluded that a system of national education for poor children would provide these children with the insights ("common sense" in Mill's words) to refrain from having too many children themselves (Mill,

1848; Weeks, 2014). Hence, the idea of cognition-driven DT that will be explicated in the next chapter has its roots in Mill, if not in Plato who also emphasized the importance of education for social stability.

A more explicit definition of the concept of DT as we still use it today is attributed to three founding fathers who came up with very similar ideas, presumably without knowing of each other's work (Kirk, 1996). In 1929, Warren Thompson specified three types of countries with different demographic regimes resulting in different patterns of population growth depending on their fertility and mortality levels (Thompson, 1929). In 1934 Adolphe Landry published "la Révolution Démographique" in which he defined three stages of demographic revolution – in the early years, both the terms *transition* and *revolution* were used – evidently without being familiar with the writings of Thompson. And he gives a much fuller description of the process and explanation of the drivers of this process that he thought would eventually take over the entire world. Unlike later writers on demographic transition Landry (1934) did not foresee an eventual equilibrium state at the end point of DT but rather envisioned depopulation with Europe facing population decline in spite of prosperity.

Today, the most widely referenced father of demographic transition theory is Frank Notestein (1902–1983) who also translated his views on demographic transition into numerical population projections for many countries around the world (Notestein, 1944). He projected that the populations of Western and Central Europe would peak around 1950 and thereafter decline. He had not anticipated the post-war baby boom and increasing international migration. He also projected that the total world population in 2000 would be 3.3 billion. Given that it turned out to be 6.1 billion shows that he greatly underestimated the mortality decline and overestimated the fertility decline over the second half of the century. While he mostly saw changing socio-economic conditions as the drivers of demographic transition, he also stated that "education and a rational point of view became increasingly important" (Notestein, 1953, p. 13). This can also be seen as an early expression of the view of a cognition driven demographic transition.

Today, DT is widely recognized in the social sciences as an established fact and also forms the basis of virtually all international population projections and thus our thinking about the future of humanity. But what

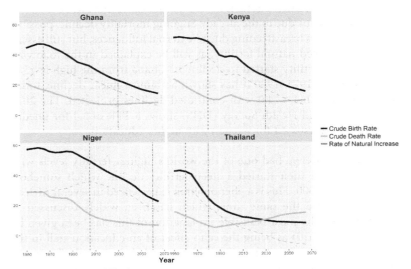

Source: WIC Data Explorer.

Figure 2.5   Demographic transitions in Ghana, Kenya, Niger and Thailand. Time series of birth and death rates (per 1000) and rates of natural increase (5-year averages)

1958 assumed essentially constant fertility rates until 1980, which was the projection horizon, although the actual TFR in 1980 turned out to be only half that level, around 3.0. In this study, there is an interesting discussion on this constant fertility assumption because the demographers at the time were well aware of DT as a predictive theory but they did not feel confident enough to assume that the onset of a fertility transition would happen within their projection horizon. While they assumed a continued mortality decline, they called the assumption of constant high fertility a "conservative assumption" (United Nations 1958 cited in Khan & Lutz, 2008). In this context, conservative turned out to be the worst assumption. Perhaps a more elaborate theory of demographic transition and more empirical information about the drivers of fertility decline – female education in Thailand had rapidly improved among the youngest cohorts over the 1950s – could have helped to produce a more accurate projection.

Ghana shows the interesting phenomenon of some increase in birth rates shortly before the onset of the fertility transition, which has also been observed in many other countries. An explanation of this can be found in better health status due to the already ongoing mortality decline, possibly together with less breastfeeding due to external influences, but still essentially uncontrolled natural fertility, as will be explained in the following section. Once fertility started to decline in Ghana from the high level of a TFR of 6.7 in 1975–1980 it has shown an almost linear decline, today reaching a level below 4.0 with continued declines projected. The 2019 Demographic and Health Survey (DHS) shows a TFR of 5.4 for uneducated women versus 2.1 for women with higher education.

Around 1970, Kenya had one of the world's highest fertility levels with a TFR of 8.1. It then started a steep fertility decline which somehow stalled around 2000. This is a phenomenon experienced in several African countries around the same time, which has been widely discussed in the literature. The most plausible explanation of this has been given by Kebede et al. (2019) as being the echo effect of an education stall in the 1980s due to economic turmoil and the so-called structural adjustment programs, which resulted in diminished budgets for education and a stall in the improvement of school enrollment for the cohorts that were in prime childbearing ages around 2000. Since female schooling has picked up again in the countries concerned – at least up until recently – the fertility decline has also gained speed again and today the TFR in Kenya is already below 3.5 (still 6.5 for uneducated women and 2.0 for those with higher education).

Niger has not really started its fertility transition yet, with the TFR still being above 7.0, after minor initial declines from around 8.0. However, death rates have already fallen to low levels with life expectancy at birth having increased from 40 in 1980 to around 60 currently. In addition, the DHS data show that the TFR of highly educated women is around 3.5, indicating a potential for fertility decline once female education, reproductive health services, and social development in general, take off. But given the current strengthening of fundamentalist Muslim groups in the country with girls being excluded from schools and madrasas replacing the weak government school system this is far from being certain for the near future.

The irreversible transition from natural fertility to parity-specific fertility control

Over the years there has also been a lot of criticism of the concept of demographic transition because of its vagueness and lack of specificity as to the precise sequence and timing of trends. On the other hand, where authors have tried to be more specific in terms of defining a clear sequence of four to five distinguishable phases of the transition, critics have always pointed at exceptions of countries or groups of countries that have not followed this specific sequence of phases. While there is no space here to summarize the decades-long discussion about demographic transitions and whether it only is a generalization of past trends or does indeed have predictive power, we will focus here on the heart of the matter, which is the question of whether the demographic transition is irreversible. This aspiration is less ambitious than the futile attempt to specify a precise sequence of stages with certain fertility and mortality levels and possibly even a typical timing of trends.

While most authors writing on demographic transition have taken the irreversibility of the fertility transition for granted, this proposition – which ultimately makes the demographic transition model a theory – is not self-evident and requires serious consideration. In this context, a recent skeptical contribution by Burger and DeLong (2016) is a welcome contribution to the discussion. They argue primarily from an evolutionary perspective that there are several reasons to assume that the fertility decline may be not permanent and thus fertility rates might well go up again in the future. One of their arguments is that fertility decline is a function of sufficient resources for modernization and if these resources (or the associated energy use) per person decline in the future due to ecological or other limits fertility could increase again. This view on fertility trends is clearly not a new concept and it has actually been at the heart of the famous classic 1972 "Limits to growth" study of the Club of Rome (Meadows et al., 1972). In their global simulation model, called World3, which was the mother of all following global systems models, they had clearly specified functions which endogenously determine the evolution of death and birth rates as a function of trends in economic growth (output), resource availability (food and oil) and pollution. Birth rates were only modeled as a function of output per person with fertility declining as output increases and fertility increasing again in the case of output falling. Since the model projected a major global crash – mostly due to resource constraints and pollution – around 2017 (with some variation of the timing depending on different assumptions) the model predicts rapidly increasing birth rates for the time after 2017 as a consequence of declining resources per person. The notion of an irreversibility of the fertility transition which was already widely held among demographers at the time seemed to be unknown to the authors of this model.

The theoretical grounding on which the irreversibility assumption of the fertility transition rests, operates at a deeper level than just the overall levels of birth or fertility rates. The theoretical grounding refers to changes in the age profiles of fertility, which reflect the emergence of parity-specific fertility control, something that has also been termed *family limitation* and was developed in the 1960s–1970s by Henry (1961) and later by the Princeton European Fertility Project (Coale & Trussell, 1974; Coale & Watkins, 1986). In this concept the fertility transition is not defined in terms of changes in overall fertility levels but as the transition from natural, i.e. uncontrolled, fertility to parity-specific fertility control. Parity in demography denotes the number of births a woman has already experienced in her lifetime (from Latin *partus* = birth), and parity-specific fertility analysis studies the rates of having an additional birth for women of different parities. The essence of parity-specific fertility control is that women stop having additional births once a certain parity is reached. As will be shown in the following, this does not translate 1:1 to lower overall fertility rates.

According to Henry's (1961) definition, in a natural fertility regime, an additional birth does not depend on parity, i.e. the number of births the woman already had. While this is a clear and straightforward definition, the empirical assessment of natural fertility through observed data is not trivial. In empirical assessments, the age-specific fertility schedule of married Hutterite women is typically taken as the standard. The Hutterites are an Anabaptist religious group that migrated from Bohemia and Lower Austria to North America and, while benefiting from modern living standards and healthcare, for religious reasons does not practice any fertility control in the form or either modern or traditional contraception. They also practice hardly any breastfeeding and therefore have short birth intervals. As a result, they were considered to have the highest marital fertility rates of any population observed. The restriction to married women in this analysis is an approximation of capturing only women who experience regular intercourse and therefore exposure to the possibility of a conception and pregnancy.

Figure 2.6 shows that even Hutterite marital fertility rates were far below the theoretical maximum fertility for mostly biological reasons. One birth every year has been considered a purely theoretical maximum fertility. There are of course many empirical examples of some women having birth intervals of only 12 months, which is in part attributable to differential fecundability (defined as the monthly probability of conception for women with regular intercourse). It is often assumed that the average waiting time to conception is around 5 months, which results from an average fecundability of 0.2. Figure 2.6 shows that 1000 married Hutterite woman in the age group 20–24 have, on average, 550 children per year. This means that the average birth interval is a bit less than two years. The different reasons why even the birth rates of young married Hutterite women are so far below the purely theoretical maximum are also listed in the figure. They include intrauterine mortality, postpartum amenorrhea and ovulations without conception. The picture also shows that for higher age groups of married Hutterite women, the fertility rates clearly fall with age. The main reasons here are early onset of sterility and possibly intrauterine mortality increasing with age. On average, Hutterite women in the 1950s had around nine children each, which is indeed the highest fertility measured for any sizable population.

The figure also plots the marital fertility curves of two other natural fertility populations with very different patterns of total fertility. The Dobe !Kung hunter and gatherer population in the Kalahari is another famous population in demography (Howell, 1979). It has the lowest natural fertility documented in the literature. With a TFR of 4.6 it has just about half of the fertility level of the Hutterites, yet there is no parity-specific fertility control, which is shown by the outward bent (concave) curve of age-specific fertility rates. In particular, the Dobe !Kung fertility of young married women is less than half that of young Hutterite women. The reason for this is labeled "C" in the figure and refers to extended birth intervals through prolonged breastfeeding or abstinence. Hunter and gatherer populations do indeed have almost universally patterns of extended breastfeeding that can be up to 4–5 years. There is clear medical evidence that a frequent suckling of the child produces larger quantities of the hormone prolactin which, under conditions of rather poor nutritional status, serves as a rather effective contraceptive. The plausible evolutional

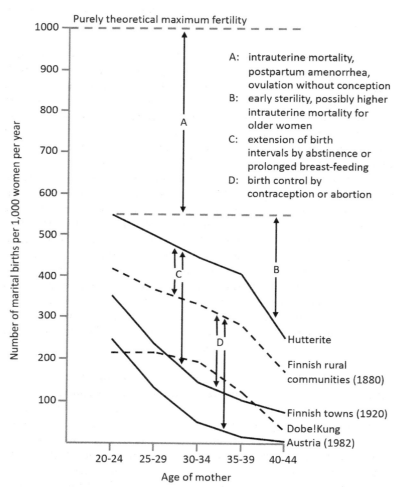

Source: Lutz (1989).

Figure 2.6   Schema depicting different reasons why observed age-specific marital fertility is lower than theoretical maximum. Examples for selected populations

reason for this is the fact that owing to the extensive walking done by these populations, the youngest child needs to be able to walk by itself for longer distances before a new baby can be carried by the mother. The data show indeed the average birth interval for the Dobe !Kung women is indeed 4–5 years. The curve only declines very slowly with age, resulting in this concave shape.

The figure also shows two populations with clearly inward bent curves. Married women living in Finnish towns in 1920 had at a young age much higher fertility than young Dobe !Kung women and only slightly lower fertility than women in the rural communities of Finland in 1880, which still had clearly natural fertility. But then, by age 30–34, fertility rates dropped lower than that of Dobe !Kung women of the same age, thus producing the convex curve. This additional source of lower fertility is due to birth control (labeled "D" in the figure). This results in the interesting fact that, overall, the natural fertility of the Dobe !Kung turned out to be lower than the clearly controlled fertility in Finnish towns in 1920. A similar pattern of controlled fertility at a still much lower level can be observed in modern Austria as in most other European countries.

To quantitatively assess when a population moves from natural to controlled fertility, Coale and Trussell (1974) developed the index of family limitation. It is an index measuring, for each age-group, the deviation from Hutterite fertility in the same age group, and distinguishes between a scale factor M and a factor m measuring the degree of control of fertility resulting from an increasing difference with age to the Hutterite level. For the above-described urban Finnish population, m stayed below 0.2 until 1900 and then increased to 0.61 in 1920 and 0.99 in 1930. In the rural communities it stayed below 0.2 until 1920, showing a rapid increase thereafter (Lutz, 1987). This index can help to assess the timing of the transition from natural to controlled fertility.

Once we have defined the theoretical concept of family limitation and its empirical measurement, the next question is whether the transition from uncontrolled fertility to family limitation is irreversible. The short answer is "yes". However, this answer needs to be qualified with respect to possible extreme cases of population heterogeneity combined with reductions in educational attainment.

The discussion of mechanisms brings us to the premises introduced at the beginning of this section combined with the first of Ansley Coale's (1973) famous three preconditions for a lasting fertility decline, namely that fertility must be within the calculus of conscious choice (these preconditions will be discussed in more detail in Chapter 3). Accepting that indeed "literacy and improved cognitive abilities through education enhance abstract thinking and foresight and reduce unplanned behavior including health and reproduction related behavior" (Proposition 5), an increasing proportion of women of reproductive age who have a minimum level of education (Propositions 1–4 as specified for DM) will lead to a higher proportion of women for which fertility is within the calculus of conscious choice and who thus move from uncontrolled fertility to parity-specific fertility control.

However, both theoretical reasoning and empirical evidence suggest that this transition to conscious family limitation is as much based on social learning as it is on individual rationality. This is where the proposition comes into play stating that "individuals are in their views, values and priorities influenced by other individuals around them depending on their proximity and attractiveness/social status" (Proposition 7). This is fully in line with the findings of the Princeton European Fertility project, which highlights cultural dissemination as a key mechanism of the transition to family limitation. In the 1990s and 2000s there was a significant body of literature focusing on social interaction, social learning and diffusion processes in the transition to family limitation (Bongaarts & Watkins, 1996; Kohler, 2001). The US National Research Council even dedicated a special report to this topic of "Diffusion processes and fertility transition" (National Research Council, 2001), which focuses on the behavioral innovation associated with the transition to family limitation. And such behavioral innovation, once it has reached the majority of the younger adult population, is assumed to be irreversible.

Can the prediction of irreversibility of the transition to family limitation be falsified through an example of a country that has passed through the fertility transition and then through exceptional circumstances, such as falling into deep poverty, moving back to uncontrolled fertility? A possible candidate for this is the Republic of Moldova which today is considered the poorest country of Europe, with rural Moldavian women having no higher income levels than many rural African women. However, as a member republic of the Soviet Union, Moldova has gone through the fertility transition, with the TFR falling to 2.4 by 1990. This was directly associated with a massive improvement of female education from 1950 – when 84 percent of reproductive age women (aged 20–39) had never been to school – to 1990 – when 65 percent of women of that age had completed upper secondary or higher education. For the late 1980s estimates of the Index of Family Limitation had been produced for all Soviet Republics (Lutz et al., 1993). The Index for Moldova is 1.68, which indicates controlled fertility with a wide prevalence of parity-specific fertility control and family limitation. After the collapse of the Soviet Union, Moldova fell into deep poverty. A fertility function that makes the birth rate dependent on income in both directions, as assumed in the above described "Limits to Growth" study of the Club of Rome (Meadows et al., 1972), would have predicted a steep increase in fertility as a consequence of this rapid decline in income. But observed trends showed the opposite. The TFR entered a further steep decline to the very low level of 1.24 in 2000–2005. This fertility response clearly confirms the prediction of irreversibility. For women before the transition to conscious family limitation, high poverty can slow the fertility decline, but once fertility has come into the calculus of conscious choice, stressful economic conditions tend to result in postponement of births and further fertility decline.

Another possible cause of a reversal of the fertility transition could be strong heterogeneity in the population, with one sub-group having very high fertility and therefore, over time, gaining in weight and possibly dominating the other low fertility groups. Israel might be an example of this where, despite a high level of education, the total TFR is rather high, around 3.0, with some groups of ultra-orthodox Jews having 4–5 children on average (Shalem, 2018). Other examples are small religiously fundamentalist groups, such as the Laestadians in Northern Scandinavia and groups similar to the Hutterite in North America. Since they do not practice family limitation as a matter of principle they can be classified as not yet having experienced the fertility transition even though they live in countries in which the majority of the population has concluded the transition. But experience shows that in free modern societies a certain proportion of the children from such religious groups do not follow the strict anti-contraception rules and enter the fertility transition. As discussed in a book on this topic, entitled *Shall the Religious Inherit the Earth?* (Kaufmann, 2011), while it cannot be ruled out that such extremist – with respect to family limitation – groups eventually take over entire populations, it seems rather unlikely, at least judging from the global level experience of the past decades.

Is the mortality transition irreversible?

The trends in mortality, as measured by the crude death rate (CDR) or age-specific mortality rates that through life table methods can be translated into period life expectancies, have been more diverse and more gradual, making it thus more difficult to define a clear-cut transition separating two qualitatively distinct mortality regimes, such as the appearance of parity-specific birth control for fertility. But still it is possible and meaningful to distinguish between early phases of mortality decline where the decline has been disproportionately concentrated among children and later phases when child mortality has already been low and the decline was more concentrated among adults. Alternatively, the notion of an epidemiological transition focuses on the changing pattern of causes of death with the original dominance by infectious diseases being gradually replaced by a pattern in which most people die of chronic/degenerative diseases. Finally, one can try to focus on the amplitude of the annual variations in death rates which have significantly declined over the course of demographic transition. However, as we will see below, there are problems with these classifications.

One further important aspect that distinguishes the drivers of the mortality transition from that of the fertility transition is the important role of disembodied knowledge about the bio-medical processes in the form of public health policies and the medical profession. A lasting mortality decline thus goes beyond changes in individual behavior and requires a strong institutional component, as has been specified in Proposition 6 above: "Individuals empowered through literacy and education can collaborate to advance the frontier of knowledge and technology and improve public health and the quality of institutions in general". This important role of knowledge, medical technology and public health institutions will be discussed in detail in the following chapter on the drivers of mortality decline.

Here, it suffices to say that any possible classification of the different stages of the mortality decline, and any definition of cut-off points, would seem a bit arbitrary. Looking at the longest historical time series for Finland, in Figure 2.3, there seems to be rather stable level in the CDR with a great degree of short-term fluctuations until the great famine of 1868, after which a marked decline starts, which is also characterized by weaker short-term fluctuations. But looking at the trend in child mortality separately shows that there had been a declining tendency since the 1750s, which then accelerated during the first half of the 19th century to around 17 percent after having been around an average of 23 percent in the mid-18th century (Lutz, 1987). However, the picture of the overall trend is distorted by the disaster of 1868 when the infant mortality rate rose to almost 40 percent. Hence, the declining trend after 1870, with reduced fluctuations, does look like a new mortality regime. But without the extraordinary events of 1869 one might have set the beginning of the new regime at an earlier stage. In the case of Mauritius in Figure 2.4, there seems to be an even more pronounced regime change in 1946–1949 associated with the end of the Second Word War and the introduction of Western medicine, including antibiotics and, in particular, malaria eradication (Lutz, 1994). However, a closer inspection of mortality trends between 1918 and 1940 shows that death rates and, in particular, child mortality had indeed fallen to unprecedented low levels during the 1920s. Again, it is not self-evident where to draw a line marking an irreversible transition.

In addition, the widely used concept of an Epidemiologic Transition (Omran, 1971) which already carries the notion of "transition" in its name is not really helpful with respect to assessing irreversibility. It refers to the shift in cause of death patterns from primarily infectious diseases to primarily chronic/degenerative ones, which is taken as a given in much of the literature on mortality (Caldwell, 2001; Vallin & Meslé, 2004) and there is an overwhelming body of empirical support for this shift for most countries in the world over the past decades. But even if the descriptive record of this shift from infectious to chronic diseases is impressive, does it provide a basis for assuming that infectious diseases will never return to dominate mortality patterns? The HIV/AIDS pandemic provides a powerful counter-example with an estimated 25–35 million people having died of it so far and with deaths disproportionally concentrated in some countries in Sub-Saharan Africa. In Botswana, for instance, in 1985–1990 the epidemiological transition had been well advanced with life expectancy at birth being above 60 years when HIV/AIDS started to dominate mortality patterns, with male life expectancy falling to 47 years by 2005–2010. In addition, the current Covid-19 pandemic reminds us that infectious diseases are far from being defeated. Finally, with a view to the longer term future Vaclav Smil (2005) provides a far-reaching overview of some of the greatest threats that humanity may face, and the possibility of a new catastrophic influenza pandemic figures among the most serious threats.

Even though it is difficult to argue for an irreversible transition in terms of the prevalence of infectious diseases or even the diminishing amplitude in short-term mortality fluctuations, virtually no one would expect a possible return to 18th century mortality conditions. This has to do with a presumably irreversible gain in scientific knowledge about the causes of disease and its treatment. The germ theory of disease has contributed to saving millions and millions of lives and it is here to stay. It is virtually unthinkable that humanity would revert back to conditions under which this theory and much of the following progress in micro-biology and medicine could be forgotten. It is thus the irreversibility in the knowledge base of humanity that is the basis for the assumption of the irreversibility of the mortality transition. This topic will be picked up again in the following chapter on cognition-driven DT.

As a postscript to this section of DT, it should be noted that in the literature there have also been discussions about what has been labeled a second and even a third demographic transition. The concept of a second DT as proposed by Ron Lesthaeghe and Dirk van de Kaa focuses on changing patterns of partnership and parenthood outside marriage (Lesthaeghe, 2014) as driven by essentially cultural change relying on Maslow's theory of shifting needs. It is labeled as "demographic" because it attempts to explain further fertility declines after the replacement level is reached, which in their view is the end of the first DT. Since, under the broader definition of DT given in this chapter, there is no artificial end to DT postulated when reaching replacement and the focus is directly on cognitive change, which includes value changes, there seems no need to distinguish between a first and a second DT but both are seen as part of a broader transformation process. Finally, the idea of a third DT as postulated by David Coleman (2006) refers to the changing composition of the population by ethnicity in the late stages of demographic transition in cases where low fertility is associated with high immigration rates of people from different ethnicities. While here the label "demographic" is clearly appropriate since it directly refers to the changing composition of populations, the focus is limited to Europe and North America and thus the concept does not claim universality and is more a categorization than a theory with predictive power. Substantively, the consequences of low fertility and immigration for the receiving countries will be the focus of Chapter 4.

The theory of a demographic dividend

In a nutshell, the theory of demographic dividend predicts that changes in demographic structures which lead to improving educational attainment of the working age population together with a higher proportion of the working population in the total population lead, on average, to increases in human well-being in economic and broader terms.

While the notion of demographic dividend has become very popular over the past years and is included in most policy documents dealing with population and development in the context of the United Nations Population Fund, the Word Bank as well as many international and national donor agencies, it has, to my knowledge, never before been framed as a demographic theory with predictive power. One reason for this may lie in the fact that the concept of demographic dividend as presented here is broader than the conventional concept which primarily focused on changes in the age structure of a population – in particular, an increasing proportion of the working age population – which was shown to be conducive to economic growth, but only if certain other preconditions are being met. The multi-dimensional demographic approach underlying this book also considers improving educational attainment structures as demographic changes that, together with age structure changes, are more powerful predictors of economic growth.

Building on the seven propositions introduced for the previously discussed demographic theories it only needs one further proposition to also cover the concept of demographic dividend.

Proposition 8: *Different members of any population are economically productive to different degrees depending on their labor force participation and their level of education/skills. An increase in the proportion of more productive people increases the potential for economic growth.*

Comment: This framing of the concept of demographic dividend makes it in my view a theory with predictive power that potentially could also be falsified, although it only predicts the potential for economic growth that may not be realized in the case of adverse institutional or other factors that limit the realization of this potential. Before we discuss the underlying mechanisms and the empirical assessment in more detail, we should have a look at the long history of the discussions around the effects of demographic trends on economic growth.

Malthus versus Condorcet and the neo-classical model

Since the theory of a demographic dividend directly addresses the effects on population changes on economic growth, this is the place to step back and have a short summary of the history of discussions around this contested relationship that has been at the heart of population theory for over two centuries.

Based on environmental, economic, social and empirical justifications, economists and social thinkers have been debating with pessimistic, optimistic and neutralist views on the impact of population growth with no strong scientific consensus (National Research Council, 1986). Thomas Malthus, in the first edition of *An Essay on the Principle of Population* (Malthus, 1798), provided the most basic description of the relationship between population and living standards. He postulated that whenever population size is relatively small and food availability is above subsistence level, "the passion between sexes" – resulting in earlier marriage and higher marital fertility – would cause a temporary rise in population size. However, since populations grow faster than food production, population pressure will continuously degrade living standards to subsistence level. The Malthusian theory predicts that unless "preventive checks" (such as "moral restraint", late marriage, and celibacy) are put in place, population size will eventually exceed the "carrying capacity" of the Earth and that "positive checks" (such as famine, disease and war) will keep the population in balance with food supply, the condition known as the "Malthusian trap".

The writings of Malthus were partly a reaction to the optimistic views on human progress expressed by the Marquis de Condorcet a few years earlier in his influential book entitled *Sketch for a Historical Picture of the Progress of the Human Mind* (Condorcet, 1795). Condorcet believed firmly in the empowerment of people through education and in particular in the strengthening of gender equity and status of women through female education. He was also an optimist with respect to technological advance and believed that technology-based improvements in efficiency can well keep pace with population growth. Condorcet thus saw prosperity and population hand in hand, and if the limits to growth were ever reached, the final solution would be birth control (Weeks, 2014). Seeing continued education and the resulting social and technological progress as the ultimate source of increases in human well-being, Condorcet in a way was an 18th century ancestor of the theory of DD as presented here.

The reasoning of Malthus was rejected on other grounds as well.[5] Karl Marx firmly dismissed Malthus' conclusions of a "natural" tendency of population growth when food is available above subsistence level, as well as the negative consequences of population pressure on economic welfare. For Marxists, poverty, unemployment and social disorders are not the direct consequence of population growth. It is the "unjust economic system" (capitalism) which is responsible not only for poverty and unemployment but for rapid population growth. Capitalists maximize profits by employing more and more capital-intensive technologies, which will gradually displace workers and reduce job availability. With the increasing surplus labor ("reserve army of labor"), wages tend to go down and poverty and unemployment prevail among the poor, while the rich can exploit more. In this view, the capitalist system promoted the "necessary" population growth by creating surplus unemployed labor and impoverished industrial workers, whose birth rates remain high (Marx, 2002).

The neo-classical economists, with a different reasoning than the Marxists, also assign population growth a neutral role with respect to economic growth. As illustrated in the famous Solow–Swan model of economic growth (Solow, 1956; Swan, 1956), unlike Malthusians the neo-classical economists do not see technology and physical capital as fixed. Through saving and investment, the pool of physical capital of a country is expandable and the faster growth of the capital stock results in growing output per capita, avoiding the "Malthusian catastrophe". Under a constant savings rate, higher population growth would cause "capital dilution" and output would fall below "equilibrium" level. However, given a well-functioning market, capital and labor can easily be substituted to keep per capita output at an equilibrium level. Thus, apart from level effects, the neo-classical growth model predicts no relationship between population growth and growth in output per-capita once – after transitory changes – a new balanced growth equilibrium is established. In the absence of technological progress, under this model there is no economic growth at all.

Following the end of the Second World War, the unexpected and unprecedented steep mortality declines in most parts of Asia coupled with still high fertility rates resulted in what Paul Ehrlich (1968) referred to as a "global population explosion". This unprecedented population growth sparked a new wave of debates on its possible consequence. According to Ehrlich, Earth has already reached its carrying capacity and "we are living with a borrowed time". Resonating with Malthus, he warns that overpopulation and the subsequent resource depletion will lead to famines, disease, war, and eventually hundreds of million people will have already starved to death by the 1970s. In a more sophisticated economic model, Coale and Hoover (1958) had already suggested, 10 years earlier, that high population growth resulting in a younger population negatively affects economic growth by reducing capital intensity. In this view, population growth forces both families and society to spend large fractions of their income on presumably less productive sectors, such as housing, education and health, and reduces the financial resources available for "more productive" investments.

In sharp contrast to this pessimistic reasoning, other scholars saw many advantages of population growth. In the neo-classical sprit, "population optimists" provide demand side and supply side arguments to defend the idea that population is an asset rather than a burden (Boserup, 1965; Kuznets, 1967; Simon, 1981). On the demand side they argue that demographic pressures promote productivity and innovations in the use of land and labor by putting pressures on scarce resources in the view that "necessity is the mother of invention" (Boserup, 1981). Boserup points at instances where high population density on a given territory triggered humankind to move through a series of increasingly intensive systems of agriculture and social organizations. These led from dispersed hunter-gatherer societies, to modern agriculture and urbanization, each system better capable of supporting a larger population. She also shows how countries with high population density have more irrigation, use chemical fertilizers, and practice more productive crop rotation, etc. Similarly, on the supply side, population optimists argue that people are not only "labor" but also creators and innovators. As Julian Simon (1981) mentioned in his book, *The Ultimate Resource*, the key to achieving and maintaining welfare is human knowledge, and its stock and efficiency increases with population size. As population increases, so does the stock of problem solving ideas and inventions. In addition, since ideas can be shared at zero cost, new ideas are developed and used more effectively in larger populations (Kuznets, 1967). In line with this view of the population optimists, the chaos and disorder in many poor countries is not due to high population growth but due to inappropriate policies and institutions (Srinivasan, 1988).

Up to the mid-1980s, the scholarly and political debates on population and economic growth oscillated between these two extreme positions. Following the publication of a landmark review study by the US National Research Council (1986), which systematically compared countries' population growth rates and economic growth rates over longer periods, and did not find any discernible relationship, a third school referred to as "neutralist" gained support. This finding was soon confirmed by other empirical studies conducting cross-country regressions and finding no significant correlation between population growth and income per capita (Kelley, 1988; Kelley & Schmidt, 1995). The conclusion drawn was that population growth neither promoted nor impeded economic growth, once other factors such as quality of institutions, educational attainment, degree of openness to trade and country size are considered.

Shifting the attention from growth to changing composition

The earlier contributions by economists and social thinkers focused primarily on changes in total population size giving less attention to the possible impacts of changing population structures. To our knowledge, the first scientific contribution on the effect of age structure on the economy stems from a now mostly forgotten German economist by the name of Ernst Günther who, against the backdrop of hyperinflation and high unemployment in Germany, wrote an article entitled, "Unemployment by Declining Birth Rates?" (Günther, 1931). Becoming significantly more prominent was the above-cited model by Coale and Hoover (1958) which is at least partially based on age-structural concerns.

More recently, there has been a revival of studies on demographic explanations of economic growth, this time with a focus on the effects of changing population structures (Prskawetz et al., 2007). While a first set of studies primarily focused on the effects of changing age structures on economic growth, another set of studies added education and labor force participation structures to the analysis. We will only summarize the first set of studies on the effects of changing age structures and discuss the subsequent strain of research focusing on education structures in more detail.

The main argument for the effect of changing age structure on economic growth refers to the changing economic impact of an individual at different stages of his/her life cycle. Children are net consumers and high birth rates can be expected to negatively affect the economy in the short run. In the long run, however, the effect may be positive as children enter into adult age and become net producers. Bloom and Williamson (1998) argued that the net effect of population change depends on the growth in working age population relative to total population. A faster rise in working age population will positively contribute to the growth of the economy – the "demographic gift". From a cross-country regression of 78 countries, they show that the growth in working age (15–64) population has a strong positive impact on economic growth, while growth in total population has a negative impact. Applying their regression outputs to the experience of East Asian countries, they indicate that about one-third of the growth miracle of the region recorded from 1965 to 1990 is explained by the countries' rapid demographic transition, which causes a significant age structure change. The transitory feature of the changes in the age dependency ratio has also given rise to the notion of a "demographic window of opportunity" that first opens and then closes as the old-age dependency ratio starts to rise. As will be discussed below, the empirical evidence does not fully support this stylized concept.

Kelley and Schmidt (2005) decomposed the impact of demographic changes on the growth of output per capita into a "productivity effect" and a "translation effect". The "translation effect", simply reflects the fact that the dependent variable is GDP per person and when you have fewer unproductive persons this variable increases. The "productivity effect" can be measured as the growth of output per worker. A declining youth dependency also leads to more resources available to invest in children's health and education (Joshi & Schultz, 2007) and investment in infrastructure. Since then, the "productivity effect" of demographic changes has been studied in more detail. Bloom et al. (2009), using a panel of 97 countries for the period 1960–2000, examined the behavioral effects of fertility decline. They showed that a reduction in fertility substantially increases female labor force participation contributing to economic growth during the demographic transition, leaving open the reasons for such fertility decline. Another recent school of thought coined the notion of a "second demographic dividend" (Lee et al., 2003; Mason & Lee, 2007), resting on the assumption that improved life expectancy leads to larger savings and investments in productive sectors, which would stimulate economic growth. Empirical studies show, however, that this mechanism heavily depends on the established system of pension transfers (Mason & Lee, 2006; Prskawetz & Sambt, 2014).

In the most recent literature on the topic, there has been a shift towards emphasizing the importance of human capital in conjunction with age structure (Crespo Cuaresma et al., 2014; Lutz et al., 2008). The history of human capital being included in growth regressions dates back further than that. Generalizing the Solow model of economic growth, Mankiw et al. (1992) add human capital as an additional factor of production and find this augmented model to be far better at explaining country-level differences in GDP per capita. The channel through which human capital affects economic growth is through its effect on productivity. Yet this finding remained unconfirmed by subsequent research (Benhabib & Spiegel, 1994; Pritchett, 2001). The reasons are attributed to problems in correctly measuring human capital as confirmed by De la Fuente and Domenech (2006), as well as Cohen and Soto (2007) who summarize their finding in the title: "Good data, good results". Moreover, we have already discussed in the previous section, on using the demographic metabolism model, how data on age- and sex-specific educational attainment could resolve this data problem (Lutz et al., 2008).

The causal link connecting human capital and economic growth can be found on various levels. Besides the skill effect boosting economic output through the higher productivity of a better educated workforce, Benhabib and Spiegel (1994, 2005) emphasize the importance of human capital in facilitating innovation, as well as in the adoption of new technologies and, thus, the catching up to the global best practice level of technology. The theoretical foundations for their empirical findings confirm the strong effect of education and can be traced back all the way to Nelson and Phelps (1966), who hypothesized that both the accumulation and the existing stock of human capital need to be included in models of economic growth to fully account for the role of human capital. Moreover, education matters to the harnessing of a demographic dividend through its effect on a population's health status (KC & Lentzner, 2010; Olshansky et al., 2012), the build-up of growth-enhancing political institutions (Lutz et al., 2010), as well as the decline in fertility (Bongaarts, 2010; Cochrane, 1979; Cochrane et al., 1990) which in turn leads to lower youth–age dependency.

How changing age and education structures interact in producing economic growth

These recent findings pointing at the importance of accounting for the age-structure of human capital called for revisiting the notion of a demographic dividend driven primarily by shifts in age structure, as well as the inclusion of further potentially relevant sources of population heterogeneity, such as labor force participation and level of educational attainment, which can serve as catalysts of the demographic dividend. Under the title "Is the Demographic Dividend an Education Dividend?", Crespo Cuaresma et al. (2014) presented a comprehensive statistical analysis of national-level time series of the demography-related drivers of economic growth to date. They decomposed demographic trends into changes in age structure, changes in labor force participation rates, and changes in the productivity of labor as approximated by the changing educational composition of the labor force. The results imply that the successful historical examples of demographic dividend effects need to be understood in the context of the educational expansion that accompanied the changes in age structure. Econometrically, the explanation for the strong effect of age structure reported by the earlier literature can be found in the conflation of declining young–age dependency ratios with increasing educational attainment in the working age population, which tend to occur in parallel. Once human capital effects are explicitly controlled for, the remaining effect of age structure is reduced to a small translation effect. The most recent findings on the education-driven demographic dividend suggest that declining youth dependency ratios on their own, i.e. without accompanying improvements in education, have negative effects with regard to income growth (Lutz, Crespo Cuaresma, Kebede, et al., 2019).

The conventional DD model – as it is still mostly referred to in the literature and illustrated by first decreasing and then increasing age dependency ratios over the course of DT – typically views fertility decline as an exogenous trigger for an increasing proportion of the population being of working ages. This primary trigger is then assumed to lead to higher productivity and faster economic growth if certain other conditions (good governance, investments in education, etc.) are being met (model A in the schema presented in Figure 2.7). The Education-triggered DD model views the same empirically observed correlation between the proportion of the population in the working ages and higher productivity as resulting from the joint effect of higher educational attainment on fertility decline and also, independently, on higher productivity (model B in Figure 2.7).

A: Conventional Demographic Dividend Model

B: Education-triggered Dividend Model

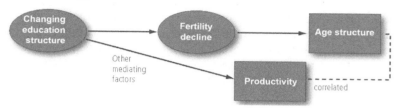

Source: IIASA (2014).

Figure 2.7   Schematic view of conventional age-structure triggered demographic dividend versus education-triggered demographic dividend

There is no doubt (and no difference between the two models in this respect) that a decrease in fertility as part of the demographic transition brings about changes in the age structure of populations which, in the short term, leads to a higher working age population as a share of the total population. However, the empirical evidence shows that this by itself does not yet trigger economic growth. Model A assumes typically that the falling proportions of children in the total population that is triggered by an exogenous fertility decline (often assumed to be a consequence of family planning programs) and the associated increasing proportions of the population of working age, creates a window of opportunity for higher growth rates of income per capita. However, this effect cannot be taken for granted, but rather depends on several enabling factors that also include investments in education. In the conventional model, the dividend disappears once the old-age dependency ratio starts to increase as a longer-term consequence to low fertility.

In contrast, the recent studies by Crespo Cuaresma et al. (2014) and Lutz, Crespo Cuaresma, Kebede et al. (2019) demonstrate the empirical validity of the alternative Model B, which assigns to education the dual role of helping to bring down fertility and enhancing productivity. In other words, in periods of expanding educational attainment, improvements in the education of women of childbearing age contribute to declining birth rates, while at the same time a more productive workforce (due to the increases in human capital) populates the labor market. The empirical analysis shows that most of the economic growth effect which, under the conventional model A is attributed to the change in age structure, turns out to be a result of the dual effect of education on fertility and productivity. Model B also provides a more optimistic outlook for the future because the strong productivity-enhancing effect of human capital does not necessarily vanish over time and even aging populations can see continued productivity growth as a function of further improving human capital, which may also be associated with higher labor force participation.

The new look at the demographic dividend described above shows that education improvement rather than an exogenous change in age structure is the gatekeeper for accessing economic growth. The econometric model that was used in Lutz, Crespo Cuaresma, Kebede et al. (2019) separates education from age-structure effects on development outcomes while also estimating the interaction terms for a panel of 165 countries for 1980–2015. The findings show that gains from a rising share of the working-age population are prevalent only when a relatively high share of the population – more than one third – is educated beyond primary schooling.

To illustrate these findings numerically, Lutz, Crespo Cuaresma, Kebede et al. (2019) also provide some numerical illustrations by comparing two countries, Nigeria and South Korea, who in 1970 had exactly the same proportion (55 percent) of their populations of working age. However, the countries were already very different in terms of the education structure and subsequently followed very different development paths. As shown in Table 2.1 even in terms of GDP per person the countries were still very similar in 1970, while by 2015 the South Korean income per

Table 2.1   Selected indicators in Nigeria and the Republic of Korea, 1970 and 2015

	Share of working age		Share with at least Junior Secondary Education		Real GDP/c, USD	
	Nigeria	Republic of Korea	Nigeria	Republic of Korea	Nigeria	Republic of Korea
1970	55%	55%	4%	18%	2393	2544
2015	53%	73%	28%	76%	5568	34,082

Source: Lutz, Crespo Cuaresma, & Gailey (2019).

person has become more than six times higher than the Nigerian income. Over the same period, the proportion of working age in South Korea had increased to 73 percent due to a rapid fertility decline, while in Nigeria it stayed roughly the same over those 45 years. GDP per person on the other hand increased by a factor of over 13 in South Korea while it only doubled in Nigeria. As the statistical decomposition analysis by Lutz, Crespo Cuaresma, Kebede et al. (2019) shows, education gains were the dominant driver of Korea's rapid income growth.

Based on the estimated set of parameters, Lutz, Crespo Cuaresma, Kebede et al. (2019) present some counterfactual scenarios as to how Nigeria would have developed under the South Korean age structure and education trends, and the vice versa. Assuming hypothetically that Nigeria had followed the same education expansion after 1970 as Korea did the simulation shows a much more rapid economic growth, which would be further reinforced if, on top of this, the South Korean increase of the share in working age is assumed. This is not surprising. What is more surprising is the fact that the statistical model shows that for very poorly educated populations an increase in the share of the population of working age without a parallel increase in education actually has a negative effect on economic growth. Hence, the counterfactual scenario that assumes that Nigeria only had the empirically observed slow expansion of educational attainment but somehow an externally induced rapid fertility decline that would result in an expansion of the share of working age population as observed in South Korea would have resulted in significantly lower economic growth than what Nigeria actually experienced. These interesting interactions between education expansion and changes in the age structure show that a fertility decline in the context of a poorly educated population is not only ineffective in pushing the development of a poor country but can even have negative impacts. The statistical model does not tell us where exactly these negative impacts come from, but it could well be related to what has been labeled the danger associated with the "youth cohort", i.e. a relatively big but unsatisfied cohort of young adults who can cause violence and institutional instability when they are neither gainfully employed nor busy with raising children. This particular issue clearly deserves more research in the future because it is politically very relevant for a large number of developing countries.

Of course, a counterfactual simulation that isolates age structure and education trends must be interpreted with caution since, in reality, the two are not independent of each other; for instance, a strong fertility decline is unlikely to take place in the absence of education. But this study leaves no doubt about the importance of education on economic growth. It is also fully in line with an elaborate body of economic theory and empirics where the importance of human capital for long run economic growth has been demonstrated by several economists during the last years within the framework of unified growth theories (Galor, 2011).

Another recent study by Kotschy et al. (2020) critically addresses the same question with a slightly different model that does not explicitly include labor force participation in the model, as the model by Lutz, Crespo Cuaresma, Kebede et al. (2019) does. It comes up with rather similar results but gives it a somewhat different twist by entitling it "The demographic dividend is more than an education dividend". This is indeed true for the general pattern derived from the set of countries and time periods for which the models have been estimated and in line with the results described above, which highlighted the synergies between simultaneously changing age- and education structures. But the Kotschy et al. paper also makes a rather strong general statement saying: "A minimum level of education is indispensable for economic growth, as is a sufficiently large working-age population share" (Kotschy et al., 2020, p. 1). Can this be seen as the predictive power of the theory of DD?

As stated at the very beginning of this section, the theory of DD predicts that improving educational attainment together with a higher proportion of the working population in the total population lead, on average, to increases in human well-being in economic and broader terms. In these rather general terms the predictive power of the theory is supported by all of the above mentioned studies and it is certainly not falsified by empirical evidence so far.

But the above-cited claim that there are minimum levels for both education and the share of the working age populations that are indispensable for economic growth goes beyond the claim of general average relationships, to claim that there should be no exceptions, as is implied by the term "indispensable". This can best be tested by looking at some unusual countries that fall out of the general patterns, which could be countries with unusually high fertility for their level of economic development or countries for which economic growth was driven almost entirely by natural resources and, in particular, oil – such as Saudi Arabia or Equatorial Guinea. Both countries did indeed show significant growth in GDP per capita over the past few decades. In addition, all countries show significant increases in the mean years of schooling of the entire adult population (MYS15+) – an indicator that is not endogenous to contemporary economic growth because the schooling of the adults had taken place decades before the economic growth is assessed – but at different levels: in Israel, the MYS15+ increased from 6.85 in 1970 to 11.6 in 2020, in Saudi Arabia from 2.48 to 10.21 and in Equatorial Guinea from 2.35 to 7.90 over the same period. Hence, significant increases in educational attainment can be confirmed for all three countries. For the total dependency ratio (TDR) – the share of non-working age population as the share of total population – the picture looks quite different. In Israel, the TDR stayed virtually constant from 0.65 in 1970 to 0.66 in 2020, which is mostly due to unusually high fertility as well as already advanced aging in the more recent years. In Saudi Arabia the TDR did decline from 0.91 in 1970 to 0.42 in 2020 due to a decline in the youth dependency ratio. And in Equatorial Guinea the TDR first increased from 0.66 in 1950 to 0.95 in 2000 and declined to 0.68 by 2020. Interestingly, the major boost in economic growth was just around 2000 when the TDR was particularly high. But one can argue that economic growth that is mostly driven by oil revenues should not be used for such a test. This leaves us with the more convincing case of Israel, where one can well claim that increasing education has been an important driver of economic growth while the share of the working age population stayed constant at a low level.

Some people may wonder why a dividend primarily derived from changes in the educational composition of populations is termed a DD. As discussed in the first chapter, this question is a consequence of demographic change sometimes being narrowly viewed as only referring to changing age structure and not the multiple demographic structures including education structure. However, under the multi-dimensional demographic approach taken here, both changes in the education structure and in the age structure, can be labeled "demographic", and both can influence the demographic dividend. Which of these demographic structural changes is more important for economic growth is a matter of empirical assessment rather than *ex ante* assumptions.

While the above discussion focused on the hypotheses of necessary preconditions for economic growth, which could be confirmed (or at least not falsified) for the case of increasing adult education and falsified for the case of age structure (at least through a couple of counter examples), one may next ask whether an improving education structure may even be a sufficient precondition. For economic growth in the narrow sense this certainly cannot be claimed since there are other institutional factors that influence the freedom of markets or other aspects that matter for the translation of increasing human capital into GDP growth. A good example for this is Cuba, where the MYS15+ are about 11 years as compared with 12 years in the USA. Yet the GDP per person in the USA is estimated to be higher by the factor of about 15 in 2000 and about 8 in 2018 (The World Bank, 2020). This can well be explained by institutional factors limiting GDP growth in Cuba. But the situation looks very different for other indicators of well-being, such as life expectancy, where male life expectancy at birth has been consistently higher in Cuba than in the USA over the past few decades. Currently, even in terms of female life expectancy Cuba has surpassed the USA.

This last example also illustrates why, in the above given specification of the theory of DD, the expected benefit is not only specified in the narrow sense of GDP per person but also in the broader sense of improving human well-being of which longevity and health are important constituents. The measurement of different aspects of human well-being and the role that improving educational attainment structures plays in its improvement over time will be discussed in subsequent chapters. This will also include the discussion of the importance of human capital for the mitigative and adaptive capacity to climate change and thus the determinants of resilience and, in the end, the enhancement of sustainable human well-being.

Toward a unified demographic theory

When bringing the three more specific demographic theories together to a unified demographic theory it is important to point at the difference between demographic theory and the long tradition of what has been called "population theory", which has been primarily concerned with the relationship between population growth and the resources necessary to sustain the life of this population. Although not entirely unrelated to the question of resources, demographic theory as understood here follows from the definition of demography as concerned with statements about changes in population sizes and structures and the way they are identified, interpreted, forecast, and understood as drivers of other relevant changes in society, economy, and the natural environment.

The question of population growth and resources for feeding the people was the central topic of Robert Malthus and his subsequent followers and critics alike, and had resulted in the concept of homeostasis, i.e. some kind of equilibrium to be reached through the adjustment of birth or death rates. The book *The State of Population Theory: Forward from Malthus* (Coleman & Schofield, 1986) cited at the beginning of this chapter comprehensively addresses this topic. The one aspect that could be added from today's perspective is the stronger awareness of environmental constraints, including the implications of global climate change. From an ecological perspective, homeostasis is primarily seen as resulting from an inevitable increase in mortality when populations surpass their carrying capacity. But how can carrying capacity, which is a useful concept for animal populations, be assessed for human populations with changing technologies? Here the authoritative book by Joel Cohen *How Many People Can the Earth Support?* (Cohen, 1996) taught us that there can be no answer to this seemingly simple question because it all depends on behavioral patterns and technologies used. While there clearly can be feedbacks from population growth to mortality at a given state of technology and in a given environment, the question makes little sense in general terms and when assessed for the very long run.

Another possible way to bring homeostasis is through fertility levels with the notion of replacement level fertility being very prominent. It is based on the undoubtedly correct statement that any upward or downward deviation from replacement level fertility (two children per woman surviving to adulthood) will in the very, very long run – and under unchanged mortality conditions – either result in unsustainable continued exponential growth or in the disappearance of the human species from earth. This thinking is also the reason why for many years the UN population projections assumed that in all countries of the world fertility levels would converge to replacement level, which together with reaching an assumed maximum level in life expectancy and no migration would result in long-term constant population sizes in all countries of the world. This view of the future also includes the assumption that in populations that are currently below this replacement level, fertility levels must eventually increase. This has been explicitly argued by Vishnevsky (1991) with reference to possible "intrinsic goals" of the demographic systems that would ultimately prevail. It assumes thus some sort of "invisible hand" in demography that goes beyond individual behavior. But very little evidence for such a possible mechanism has been found so far, except for evidence of a weak but statistically significant density-dependence of desired and actual fertility in certain settings (Lutz et al., 2007).

As said above, the theory focus of this volume is not on homeostasis and the relationship between population growth and resources, but rather on the internal dynamics of demographic changes of humans by age and cohort as well as other important demographic dimensions – such as gender, level of education, labor force participation, etc. – and the way these demographic changes influence changes in society and the economy and our relationship to the natural environment. To clearly distinguish this perspective from population theory concerned with resources in the Malthusian sense, it is called "demographic theory". In the previous sections of this chapter I introduced three distinct demographic theories based on three different traditions and bodies of literature. Already when deciding to discuss them in a non-random sequence it became clear that they build on each other: demographic metabolism covering the pattern of predictable demographic change along cohort lines, demographic transition as covering the "once in history" transition to a new demographic regime, and demographic dividend as covering the consequences of demographic changes in terms of economic growth and general human well-being.

In this section I will attempt to bring these three demographic theories together to a *Unified Demographic Theory*. I will do so by simply restating the eight Propositions that have been introduced in the previous sections as parts of the foundations of the three theories and relate them to each other.

Proposition 1: *People – individual humans – are the primary building blocks of every population or sub-population of interest and the primary agents of social and economic behavior. Hence, they form the basic elements (atoms) of any theory of aggregate-level social and economic change.*

Proposition 2: *For any population, members can be subdivided into disjoint groups (states) according to clearly specified and measurable individual characteristics (in addition to age and sex) for any given point in time.*

Proposition 3: *Over any interval of time, members of a sub-population (state) defined by certain characteristics can move to another state (associated with different characteristics), and these individual transitions can be mathematically described by a set of age- and sex-specific transition rates.*

Proposition 4: *If any given population consists of sub-groups that are different from each other with respect to relevant characteristics, then a change over time in the relative size of these sub-groups will result in a change in the overall distribution of these characteristics in the population, and hence in social change.*

These first four propositions form the backbone of the theory of demographic metabolism which captures the replacement of generations and describes analytically how societies change as a function of the changing composition of its members with respect to relevant individual characteristics. This model of cohort replacement is valid for all populations at all times. It can also be characterized as a biological law that is based on the fundamental balancing equation of demography as described in Chapter 1.

One specific "game-changing" episode in the demographic evolution of any population is the demographic transition from uncontrolled to controlled mortality and fertility. This demographic regime change has also appropriately been labeled "demographic revolution". It also builds on the replacement of generations but requires three more propositions in order to explain and predict what is happening through this unique episode in the history of every population. Proposition 5 adds the "quality dimension" to the purely compositional changes by introducing the cognitive empowerment associated with increasing education.

Proposition 5: *Literacy and improved cognitive abilities through education enhance abstract thinking and foresight and reduce unplanned behavior including health and reproduction related behavior.*

But societies change not only as a function of the changing composition of its individual members. In order to capture processes resulting from the interactions of individuals leading to the establishment of rules/institutions as well as disembodied knowledge such as scientific insights that gain momentum beyond the individuals that came up with them, the following proposition is needed, in particular with respect to the role of public health in the mortality transition.

Proposition 6: *Individuals empowered through literacy and education can collaborate to advance the frontier of knowledge and technology and improve public health and the quality of institutions in general.*

In order to capture ideational changes other than those introduced by generation replacement, one also has to address social learning that can result in changes in the views and other modifiable characteristics over the life courses of individuals. This can either be endogenized in the quantitative model and captured in terms of transition rates from one state (mindset, holding a value) to another, as described in Proposition 3, or it can be viewed as operating implicitly as something changing the average within the sub-division considered. It thus captures the diffusion of ideational change.

Proposition 7: *Individuals are in their views, values and priorities influenced by other individuals around them depending on their proximity and attractiveness/social status.*

When addressing the economic consequences of demographic change as captured in the theory of demographic dividend then in addition to Proposition 5 it has to be assumed that educated people are not only better empowered but also economically more productive when they are part of the labor force.

Proposition 8: *Different members of any population are economically productive to different degrees depending on their labor force participation and their level of education/skills. An increase in the proportion of more productive people increases the potential for economic growth.*

This concluding summary of the chapter on demographic theories has tried to pull things together from the three constituent theories of the

Unified Demographic Theory in the form of the eight propositions that provide the skeleton of this new theory based on the multi-dimensional approach to demography.

Many questions are still open in this respect. Some of them have already been addressed in the preceding sections, others will be addressed in the two subsequent chapters on the drivers of global fertility and mortality trends and the demographic aspects of sustainable development that do ultimately also influence population policy priorities. Yet, other questions will have to wait for future clarification and discussion. This presentation of the Unified Demographic Theory is only a first shot at trying to provide the discipline with a comprehensive theoretical framework that will need much further elaboration and hopefully contribute to its strengthening.

Notes

1. Although Karl Popper to my knowledge never wrote explicitly about theories in demography, I had the opportunity in the early 1980s to discuss the topic with him over a cup of tea in his house outside London in return for bringing him several packages of his favorite dish, Viennese potato goulash. Some of the views expressed here reflect this discussion.
2. This sub-section on functional causality draws in part on Chapter 2 of Lutz, Butz and KC (2014).
3. This section on demographic metabolism draws in part on Lutz (2013) and Lutz (2015).
4. This section on the demographic metabolism of European identity draws in part on Striessnig and Lutz (2016).
5. The text in the rest of this section is partly based on an unpublished manuscript on demographic dividend authored by Erich Striessnig, Wolfgang Lutz, Endale Kebede and Nicholas Gailey.

3 Education and cognition as drivers of mortality and fertility decline

In the previous chapter we introduced the three demographic theories that have been assessed to have predictive power at the aggregate level of populations. We could not discuss the theory of demographic transition and its irreversibility without referring to the drivers of mortality and fertility decline. This theory only makes sense if we have at least a vague notion of what drives the transition and its timing in different parts of the world. The traditional notion that "modernization" drives demographic transition is indeed a very vague explanation. In this chapter we will try to define in more precise terms what aspects of modernization have resulted in the historical declines of death and birth rates and are also likely to drive future changes.

Much has been written about the drivers of fertility and mortality decline. Interestingly, the discussions around the drivers of these two main demographic factors have been quite unrelated, where, with respect to mortality, the controversy was about the relative role of nutrition and economic growth on the one hand and medical progress on the other. With respect to fertility there have been three broad explanations competing with each other: socio-economic change, value change and family planning programs. There is no room here to comprehensively summarize these controversial discussions that took place over the past half century. Instead, we will introduce a new kind of explanation that can help to resolve these controversies by moving them to a different level of analysis. Rather than trying to find the cause in different external forces that determine the behavior of people, we will focus on the changes in our minds or, even more concretely, in our brains – the organ that steers all of our behavior, including health-related and reproductive behavior. We will discuss why

the basic difference between these two strains of argument as those supporting an understanding of mortality decline as a by-product of economic growth and improved standards of living, versus those that support "human agency" in the form of public health interventions and basic improvements in infrastructure as being the primary drivers of the decline (Colgrove, 2002).

More recently, medical sociologists have attempted to link socio-economic differences in mortality, pervasively observed at given points in time, with changes in both the direction and magnitude of these differences over time. This "fundamental cause theory" was developed first and most extensively by Link and Phelan (1995). At its base, it argues that economic and social resources are "fundamental" to health because they can be flexibly employed in vastly different health environments and in multiple ways to ensure health advantages for individuals of higher socio-economic status. In essence, social and economic position in society are linked to proximate determinates of health – access to preventative and therapeutic healthcare, health-related behaviors, environmental and cultural influences on health, etc. – regardless of the specificity of the disease environment and proximate determinants.

Many have criticized the fundamental cause approach for its failure to specify which aspects of socio-economic status are themselves "fundamental" for determining relative probabilities of death. There is continuing ambiguity in the specification of how specific socio-economic resources – education, material wealth, social position and its relative power to influence the conditions of life, social networks, and education – are all components of socio-economic status. Thus, much of the criticism of the fundamental cause approach mirrors the continuing debate over the demographic and epidemiologic transitions: without a clearer concept of which aspects of modernization (increasing wealth or increasing knowledge influencing health-related innovation or increasing education allowing access to that knowledge) or which aspects of socio-economic status (wealth or social position or social networks or education) do most to influence health disparities, these approaches remain primarily descriptive and irrelevant to policy formulation (Deaton, 2002; Freese & Lutfey, 2011).

What then can the literature say about advances in knowledge and education as causes of mortality decline? Cutler, Deaton, and Lleras-Muney explicitly acknowledged this connection in their article published in 2006 taking a comprehensive look at the determinants of mortality. This article begins by asserting that "… [t]he decline in mortality over time, differences in mortality across countries and differences in mortality across groups within countries are phenomena worthy of serious attention by economists and others…" and that "… a good theory of mortality should explain *all* of the facts …" (Cutler et al., 2006, p. 98; emphasis in original).

Their summary of the historical decline in mortality in Western countries divides change into three phases: (1) from the middle of the 18th century to the middle of the 19th century; (2) the later decades of the 19th century to the beginning decades of the 20th century; and (3) finally from the 1930s to the present. They conclude that while economic gains and improved nutrition may have played some role in the first phase, public health measures were likely to have also been important and these measures became the primary influencer of mortality decline in the second phase. In the third phase, the role of medicine expands "… to the expensive and intensive personal interventions that characterize the medical system today" (Cutler et al., 2006, p. 106).

In examining the mortality differences between low and high income countries, and particularly the declines in mortality that have occurred in lower income countries, the authors conclusively downplay the role of economic growth relative to public health improvements and advances in education, particularly with respect to women's education and the decline in infant and child mortality.

It is when examining the determinants of differences among social groups within countries, however, that the authors come down most heavily on the side of education being the primary determinant of mortality differences, especially as contrasted to the role of income. This conclusion acknowledges a long trajectory of research that has shown a stronger and more consistent effect for education than income (Mechanic, 2007; Mirowsky & Ross, 2003; Smith, 2007). Recent evidence on inequality of health in Europe also confirms the dominant role of education differentials, which Mackenbach (2019), after careful analysis, also attributes to a large extent to real causal effects of education rather than possible selection or third factors.

Cutler, Deaton and Lleras-Muney defend their support for the primacy of education's role in determining mortality by drawing on the evidence cited not only for the historical decline in mortality but also that of differential mortality across and within countries. In essence, they argue that "... [k]nowledge, science and technology are the keys to any coherent explanation" of observed trends and differences (Cutler et al., 2006). While acknowledging the complexity of socially determined mortality, and issuing the caveat that no single cause can be the entire explanation of such diverse changes in the structure of mortality, they nevertheless argue in favor of increasing knowledge and its application to health-related innovations as the primary factor enabling both the exercise of a degree of human control over death and generating differences in the degree with which this control is exercised. Specifically, they assert that mortality began to decline in the West only after the Enlightenment owing to the direct effect it had on ideas about personal health and hygiene and the role of public administration, as well as its indirect effect on increased productivity that helped to produce better living standards.

The above review of the literature also has made it clear that personal health and survival cannot be reduced to individual behavior as influenced by education and improved cognition. Any comprehensive assessment of the role of education must also explain how it is that even uneducated individuals can have lower mortality risks if they live in communities or societies with a high degree of knowledge and technological innovation. This community level effect that goes beyond individual empowerment has already been reflected in Proposition 6 of the previous chapter on theories addressing the role of collaboration, collective knowledge and the building of institutions. As will be seen in the following sections, this macro level effect of public health and medical progress interacts closely with individual level cognition and behavioral choices, resulting in better health outcomes and declining mortality.

Literacy and mortality decline in 19th-century Sweden

In 1751, England and Sweden had about equal life expectancies at birth of around 38 years (Schofield, 1984). France was markedly lower with 29 years as were most other European countries and presumably virtually all populations around the globe. By 1800, life expectancy in England had remained virtually unchanged while it had moderately increased in Sweden to 41 years. This advantage of Sweden over England rose to around four years by the mid-19th century. After this the increase of life expectancy in Sweden greatly accelerated reaching, for women, 50 years around 1880 and 60 years around 1920. Sweden had thus spearheaded the modern mortality decline and it is instructive to try to understand what triggered this development that kick-started the global demographic transition and changed the world and is probably the single most important progress in the history of humanity.

In economic terms, 19th century Sweden was not so different from many other European countries; actually it was still more rural than many of them. But the one respect in which it significantly differed was the level of literacy among the general population. Sweden's unique literacy history started with the Church Law of 1686, stating that all Swedes should learn to read so that they can personally understand the Bible and be individually conscious of Christian life and faith (Johansson, 2007). The religious foundation for this law was the revolutionary and egalitarian message of the Reformation which, among other things, rejected the priestly monopoly on religious scripture and godly communication. Lay people, at all levels of society were encouraged to read the Bible and discuss the religious message with clerics and family. This call for literacy of even the lowest female servants (German "Das geringste Mägdelein") was the socially revolutionary message of Martin Luther that he made for religious reasons and which had massive consequences for world development over the centuries (Lutz, 2017b).

A unique characteristic of the early literacy program in Sweden was that reading was taught at home, passed down from parents, who initially learned the skill from parish priests. Formal education for both boys and girls was not made compulsory until 1842. Moreover, the ability to read was not limited to the Bible and other religious texts. Government pamphlets related to health, nutrition and hygiene were available and read as early as the mid-18th century, with the intent of making healthcare accessible to everyone (Högberg, 2004).

There are several other aspects of literacy and education that should be considered. There are considerable analyses, particularly in the field of public health, that argue that human agency – that is, the impact of trained doctors, nurses, midwives, public health officials – has had a positive impact on health and reduced both child and adult mortality. Research on Sweden by Lundberg (2003) and Högberg (2004) among others, has pointed to human agency as an important historical phenomenon. Medicine as a profession was legalized in 1663 and the formal training of midwives began in the early 19th century. In addition, the spillover from educated individuals who were not health professionals but knowledgeable regarding health issues may have had positive effects. Contemporary work by Pamuk et al. (2011) on developing countries has shown the positive impact of educated individuals in communities.

Sweden has a unique historical database on individual level demographic data based on parish registers that have been digitalized. This database has been used to assess trends over the 19th century in the differentials in child mortality by different education groups, using the occupation of the head of household as a proxy (Sandström et al., 2016). Child mortality was by far the lowest for clergy followed by teachers, two groups that were highly educated but not particularly wealthy. On the other hand, the owners of big farms and merchants had higher child mortality levels than clergy and teachers, although they were clearly richer. Already this micro-level comparison indicates that for child mortality in 19th century Sweden education mattered more than income.

Very similar findings result from an econometric study at the aggregate level of national trends for a group of 16 countries for which data go back to 1870, and 25 more countries with data since 1910 (Murtin, 2013). This elaborate study, using several different model specifications, concludes that the effect of education on infant mortality is three times as large as that of income. For life expectancy at birth the results also show that education rather than income explains the bulk of rise in life expectancy over the 20th century.

Revisiting the Preston Curve

Since the middle of the 20th century, life expectancies at birth have shown stunning increases in virtually all countries. The global average of 46 years in 1950 has made the dramatic jump to 72 years today, with global child mortality declining from 22 percent to only 4 percent over the same period. Yet, as mentioned above, discussions of the causes of this major success, arguably one of the greatest achievements of humanity, have been controversial. A reference point for much of the analysis has been the Preston Curve (Preston, 1975), which illustrates the global relationship between GDP per person on the horizontal axis and life expectancy on the vertical over the twentieth century. This work reveals a strong but diminishing effect with increasingly higher incomes, as well as an upward shift of the curves which has been interpreted as the effect of medical progress and healthcare over and above the effect of income. Figure 3.1(A) gives this global level relationship for three curves showing data for around 1970, 1990 and 2010.

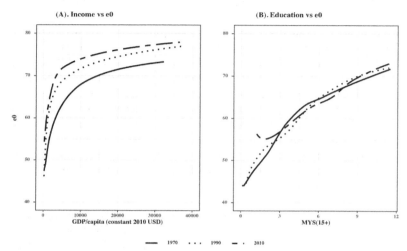

Source: Lutz and Kebede (2018).

Figure 3.1   Relationship between GDP/capita (left) and the Mean Years of Schooling of the adult population (right) to Life Expectancy at Birth (vertical axis) for all countries in the world in 1970, 1990 and 2010 (curves fitted through data points)

An alternative view claims that low mortality does not come as an unplanned spinoff from economic growth but rather results primarily from higher female autonomy associated with better education (Caldwell & Caldwell, 1985; Cutler et al., 2006). In a recent paper, Lutz and Kebede (2018) test the two opposing hypotheses with new global data as recent as 2015, finding that increasing education levels explain the observed life expectancy improvements much better than increasing income. The widely assumed direct association between income and health is interpreted as being predominantly of a spurious nature because better education has positive consequences on both higher income and higher life expectancy. Better education tends to lead to improved cognition, which in turn is associated with longer planning horizons and more conscious choices of health-related behaviors. These mental factors become increasingly important as the burden of disease shifts from infectious to chronic diseases more closely associated with lifestyle decisions.

The new study both revisits the influential Preston (1975) paper on the relationship between income and life expectancy for most countries of the world in the 1930s and 1960s, and extends the analysis to the period 1970–2015. Figure 3.1 shows that the distinct pattern identified by Preston – a strongly concave relationship and an upward shift of the curves – continued over subsequent decades. Figure 3.1(B) plots the same kind of relationship, replacing GDP per person by the mean years of schooling of the adult population. The associations turn out to be very different, with the curves becoming largely linear and overlapping. This suggests that educational attainment is a better predictor in the sense that its effect on life expectancy does not diminish at higher levels and, in particular, it does not leave an unexplained shift over time that has to be explained by other factors.

To validate this visual analysis, the study conducts multivariate analyses on a balanced panel of 174 countries for 1970–2015, which in addition to GDP per person and mean years of schooling of the adult population included country and period fixed-effects, and performed sensitivity runs with alternative income indicators and weighting schemes. In all of the models, the effect of educational attainment on life expectancy is highly significant in the expected direction, and the standardized coefficients are clearly larger than those of income.

Setting policy priorities in both developing and industrialized countries depends on answering whether income, or education, is the most important determinant of mortality decline. The answer matters for choosing between programs that directly promote income growth and others that enhance school enrollment and quality of schooling. While ideally one would promote both of these goals together with good health services, reality often necessitates choices between these priorities. Our analysis implies that investments in education and knowledge creation are more effective in reducing premature mortality.

With more education we expect fewer disabilities

With the decline in mortality and the gradual reduction of death rates in younger ages in many countries, the focus of attention is moving from avoiding premature deaths to improving the health status of the population and postponing the onset of disabilities among older people. In the context of an ever-increasing proportion of the population in older age groups there is now the widespread expectation that in the future the prevalence of disability will increase and there is a sharply rising need for care of disabled elderly. The simple reasoning underlying this expectation is that disability rates increase with age and when there are more old people there will be more disability.

Under a multi-dimensional perspective that does not attribute all the variation in disability to age and sex but also includes variations with respect to level of education, the picture looks very different. Since the data show that at any given age men and women with more education have significantly lower levels of disability and since we know for sure that the future elderly will be more educated than today's elderly, this is a force towards lower disability rates in the future working against the trend of increasing proportions of elderly. How the balance of these opposing forces can play out numerically in different parts of the world has been calculated by KC and Lentzner (2010).

Data from virtually all countries show that the risk of falling into disability and of dying at any given age varies greatly by level of education for both men and women (KC & Lentzner, 2010). For male life expectancies, these differences between the highest and lowest educational groups in various countries range from a high of 12 years in Eastern Europe to some 3–4 years in Mediterranean countries. Data from the World Health Survey[2] show that education differentials are even more pronounced for disabilities. In this survey, respondents provided information on demographic characteristics, health status, risk factors, access and utilization of health services and healthcare expenditure. KC and Lentzner (2010) studied indicators measuring disability based on responses on activity of daily living (ADL) and self-reported health (SRH).

The results show, for all world regions, that significant health differentials by level of education affect not only the elderly population beyond working age but also the working age population itself. While the first is primarily relevant for assessing the future need for care for the disabled, the latter also directly matters for the ability to work and be productive as a member of the workforce. The study by KC and Lentzner (2010) then contrasts two alternative projections up to 2050, one based on the conventional breakdown by only age and sex and one based on the multi-dimensional approach which additionally differentiates by level of education. This first projection, which only considers age and sex, indeed shows the widely expected increasing trend of disability for the future, which is simply the consequence of a projected higher proportional elderly together with the pattern that disability increases with age.

In the second set of projections, KC and Lentzner (2010) enriched the model by factoring in the education/disability relationships obtained from the WHS analysis. These multi-dimensional projections that are based on the same empirical baseline but also cover the education heterogeneity were carried out on the basis of three different scenarios on future school enrollment. The results show that even under the most pessimistic scenario that assumes constant school enrollment numbers (no new schools being built) the proportions with disabilities in the age group 30–74 actually decline in Asia, Latin America and Europe over the coming decades. For more optimistic school enrollment scenarios this decline is even stronger.

The reason for this very different result lies in the fact that in most parts of the world the young cohorts are much better educated than the older ones and therefore we know with certainty that – even under pessimistic assumptions of future school enrollment – the older adult population will be significantly better educated than today. And combined with the fact that the more educated have lower disability rates, this results in an actual decrease in the prevalence of disability, at least up to age 75 for which data are given.

In conclusion, the evidence and studies described in this section make it clear that significant differentials in health and mortality do not only exist across countries and over time but also within countries. In all these cases, differences in level of education seem to play a decisive role and turn out to be more relevant than differences in income. In terms of the implications of this for the future, it has been shown that an explicit accounting for education heterogeneity in addition to age and sex makes the future look different and makes it look more optimistic since, in most countries, a further improvement in the educational attainment structure of the population is already pre-programmed in today's age structure. This is also a good example for how a multi-dimensional demographic approach reaches very different conclusions from a narrow focus on age and sex alone.

Drivers of fertility decline

The secular transition from uncontrolled high fertility rates to conscious family limitation and consequently low fertility has been associated with fundamental changes in society that range from the rise of the nuclear family at the micro level to the changing role of women at the macro level of society, economy and politics. While the key concepts of this irreversible fertility transition have already been introduced above in the section on Demographic Transition theory, in this section we will dig deeper in terms of discussing possible alternative explanations of this highly consequential change in reproductive patterns. We will also not restrict the discussion to the once-in-history fertility transition but broaden the perspective to possible long-term levels of post-transition fertility.

Similar to the previous section, where we discussed the concept of cognition-driven mortality decline, first in terms of its beginnings in 19th century Sweden and then its spread around the world over the 20th century, here we will discuss the concept of cognition-driven fertility decline first in terms of its beginning in 19th century France and then its spread around the world with the transition in Africa still being incomplete.

The start of the fertility transition in France

The national population that for the first time in human history entered a lasting fertility decline through the adoption of widespread conscious family limitation was France. It is estimated that around 1800 the TFR of France was around 4.5 children per women, which is already slightly lower than the 4.5–5.0 registered in Finland and Sweden around the same time, as well as that estimated for other countries in Northern and Western Europe (Lutz, 1987; Sundbärg, 1907). It is widely assumed that the onset of the fertility decline in France is closely linked to the deep social upheaval associated with the French Revolution 1789–1793.

Since France does not have complete historical records comparable with those in Sweden, one has to rely on partial information and indirect estimates, such as those by the Princeton European fertility project, which shows for the beginning of the 19th century a clearly declining trend in both overall and marital fertility (Coale & Watkins, 1986). The Princeton indices show for 1831 – the first year for which these indices are given for France – the index of marital fertility was already as low as 0.537, further declining to 0.478 by 1851 and 0.383 by 1901. This index sets the above discussed Hutterite fertility as a standard of 1.0. Thus, even in the first half of the 19th century, French marital fertility was already at half the Hutterite level. This is indeed already much lower than in most other parts of Europe where the comparable indices remained mostly above 0.70 until the end of the 19th century. The average of all European provinces (excluding France) was at 0.723 as late as 1880 (Watkins, 1986). This clearly illustrates that France had a unique pivotal role in the transition to family limitation.

This early fertility decline in France has given rise to much discussion and controversy about the drivers of the onset of the global fertility transition. The French experience challenges many of the conventional explanations of fertility decline, such as being a lagged response to declining child mortality or being a consequence of urbanization or economic growth. In France, fertility started to decline under rather high infant mortality and both continued to fall almost in parallel, thus being a prominent counterexample to the often used classification of demographic transition into distinct phases where, in the early phase, only mortality declines while fertility still stays at a high level. Also, no consistent pattern has been found in which higher levels of urbanization or economic factors could have explained this French exceptionalism in fertility. In many of these socio-economic dimensions, France was not so different from the rest of Europe. The main explanation given by the Princeton Project for this lack of explanation through the conventionally assumed factors was to point at cultural and ideational factors with the French Revolution seen as the engine of secularization (Lesthaeghe, 1980).

Interestingly, one factor that was not given systematic attention in the study of the causes of the French fertility decline and the European

Fertility Project in general, is the possible role of literacy and education in triggering this development. Van de Walle, a key member of the Princeton team and expert on French historical demography, acknowledges this fact and explains it with the lack of reliable information on education. In a paper on Switzerland where good education records exist for the period of fertility decline, he actually finds a strong association between lower fertility and higher female education both across the population as well as over time (van de Walle, 1980). He concludes that education may teach people to cope more rationally with the environment and become less fatalistic and to plan more in all aspects of their lives.

Newer studies on literacy in France in the late 18th century and early 19th century indeed find increasing evidence of astonishingly high literacy especially among women. These new studies systematically assess non-demographic sources of data such as signatures on legal records of inheritance and transactions of property and find that, particularly in Northern France, significant proportions of women could already sign their names in the late 18th century. It has been estimated that, on the eve of the French Revolution, 47 percent of the total male population of France and 27 percent of the female population could read. For Northern France it is estimated that, by 1800, 44 percent of all women could read, which is likely among the highest female literacy rates of any population at the time (Lyons, 2001; Reis, 2005). Literacy continued to expand over the course of the 19th century through the provision of primary schooling and the emergence of a mass culture of print and, by the end of the century, functional literacy had become almost universal for both French men and women (Lyons, 2001). This exceptionally early spread of female literacy – only competing with the previously described case of Sweden – together with the above-mentioned push of secularization through the French revolution – which had no equivalent in Sweden – brought a unique mix of cognitive and ideational change fostering the spread of the behavioral innovation of family limitation earlier than in any other population of the world.

It is also likely that this new form of conscious reproductive behavior in increasing segments of the population could build on earlier modes of behavior among certain French elites. From the study of novels and other literary evidence it becomes quite clear that, among the higher social classes, the determination to have a particular number of children – rather than having as many as God gives – first appeared in France in the 17th century, presumably much earlier than in any other society (van de Walle, 1992).

Three pre-conditions for a lasting fertility decline

England was much later in this process although there were also differences by social class. In 1848, John Stuart Mill pointed at a clear social differentiation on this matter in British society – which presumably also reflected a difference in education levels – when he wrote about the working classes that

> ... the idea ... never seems to enter anyone's mind that having or not having a family, or the number of which it shall consist, is amenable to their own control. One would imagine that children were rained down upon married people, direct from heaven, without there being art or part in the matter. (Mill, 1848, p. 155)

This same fatalistic attitude toward childbearing described here for the uneducated groups of 19th century Britain is also reflected in modern surveys in largely illiterate communities in Africa, where high proportions of women interviewed are unwilling to give a numerical answer to the question on ideal family size. Taking the example of a qualitative survey in Bamako (Mali) in 1983, a woman answered the question of how many children she would personally want: "Oh, me. I cannot tell the number of children to God. What he gives me is good, that's enough. To say that I can stop and say the number, to tell God what to give me, I could not do so" (cited by van de Walle, 1992, p. 492).

This transition – which originated in Europe and then moved to the Americas and most of Asia and is still ongoing in Africa – from having as many children as God gives to having as many as parents want, seems to be closely linked to the spread of literacy among broad segments of the population. Today, the vast majority of the world population is already literate and has also entered into or passed through this major cognitive and cultural transition that enlightenment and modernity have brought about. And importantly this cognitive transition is not just linked to Western culture but rather a universal development that is intrinsically linked with abstraction skills that are associated with literacy and formal education also of a non-Western type. Because it is based on a real qualitative change that happens in the mind of people and not just an adjustment to changing external conditions, this transition to a conscious choice of family size is labeled here as cognition-driven fertility transition.

This cognitive transition is a necessary precondition for a lasting fertility decline, but not the only precondition. As clearly specified by Ansley Coale (1973) there are three such necessary preconditions:

1. Fertility must be within the calculus of conscious choice;
2. Lower fertility must be advantageous;
3. There must be acceptable means for preventing births.

The first precondition was discussed above. The second refers to considerations of the costs and benefits of children. While much of the extensive research on this topic focuses primarily on economic costs and benefits, more recent studies have also highlighted the importance of women's health and female status as important benefits of lower fertility. The third precondition refers to the methods by which unwanted births are being avoided. For good reasons it is formulated in a rather neutral way because what is an acceptable method may differ greatly by culture and historical context. Cultural norms with respect to the legitimacy of abortion as a method of family limitation have been very different; for example in Japan abortion was widely practiced during the fertility transition, while it was strictly forbidden – although still practiced to a certain extent – in other cultural contexts. It has been well documented that European fertility decline up until the middle of the 20th century has been mostly based on abstention and coitus interruptus, methods that would hardly be acceptable in modern European societies. For this reason it is misleading to only focus on the availability of modern contraceptive methods as a prerequisite for a lasting fertility decline, which is hardly warranted from a historical perspective.

Next, we will try to briefly summarize some key perspectives from the huge literature on different advantages of lower fertility and the costs and benefit perspectives that can lead to a choice of lower family size.

Child mortality decline as a possible trigger

It is a central narrative of conventional Demographic Transition theory that the onset of the fertility transition was triggered by an earlier decline in child mortality. Assuming that somehow parents had always been aiming at a certain number of surviving offspring, it seems plausible that the number of births needed to reach this goal declines as more of those children survive to adulthood. But both the theoretical foundations as well as the empirical support for this assumption are weak. We have already discussed above that before the introduction of conscious family limitation, parents typically did not have a quantitative goal of reaching a certain number of surviving children. Also, in historical time series, the mortality decline did not always precede the fertility decline, as with the above-described case of France. As for contemporary trends in Africa, there seems to be only weak evidence for such a mechanism, with many countries that had experienced declines in child mortality rates decades ago still showing very high fertility rates. Actually, the number of children surviving to adulthood has significantly increased in Africa due to the combined effect of continued high fertility and significantly declining child mortality over recent decades.

The empirical evidence on the temporal relationship between fluctuations in child mortality and fertility also shows an interesting change in the nature of the relationship over the course of demographic transition, as has been shown, for example, for the above-described long-time series of birth and death rates for Finland. Using cross-lagged correlation analysis it has been shown that in the early context of essentially uncontrolled natural fertility birth and death rates, both had a strongly negative association in the same year (death rates being high and birth rates being low in years of crisis) and there have been no signs of significantly higher fertility in the subsequent years to possibly make up for the deceased children. In the 20th century, however, when fertility has entered the calculus of conscious choice, clear indications for possible replacement strategies appear in annual time series data (Lutz, 1984). Similar results were found at the micro-level from studies of the 1900 and 1910 public use samples of the US census (Haines, 1998) as well as from analyses of survey data in contemporary African societies (Defo, 1998; Lindstrom & Kiros, 2007). Put in a nutshell, the evidence about a direct effect of lower child mortality on lower fertility is more complex and less convincing than the simple narrative based on a target of surviving children would suggest. While there is little empirical evidence for this in the early phases of demographic transition, in societies further advanced in the process more evidence is found, but the picture is not uniform.

Economic costs and benefits

The neoclassical economic model of fertility explains childbearing behavior as the outcome of a utility-maximizing decision made by parents in response to economic costs and benefits (Becker, 1981; Becker & Barro, 1988; Becker et al., 1990). The economic benefits from children are mainly of two types: (1) current income flows, which can consist of the imputed value of home labor, extramural earnings turned over to parents by children still resident in the household, or remittances sent by children who have left the household (Clay & Vander Haar, 1993) and (2) future old-age security. Economic costs relate mostly to the costs of education and the opportunity costs of time spent in childbearing and child care.

According to the neoclassical model, the well-being of parents – without distinguishing between the interests of mothers and fathers – is considered to be a function of "child quantity" (i.e., number of children), "child quality" (i.e., educational endowment, health, etc.), and the level of consumption of all other goods. The price of child quantity involves certain fixed but context dependent costs, such as direct expenditure for the child and time used for childbearing and rearing; the price of child quality involves costs related to education and other investments in human capital. Altruism toward future generations can also be added to the model by including well-being of the children as an additional argument in the parents' utility function (Nerlove et al., 1987).

Fertility decline, according to this neoclassical model, results from a combination of increasing costs of child quantity (such as increasing housing costs or opportunity costs through increasing employment of women in the formal sector) and declining costs of child quality (for example, increasing availability of educational opportunities). All else being equal, increases in income per person associated with economic development would lead to increases in fertility just as they lead to increases in the consumption of material goods. This is the positive income effect that would lead to higher birth rates if nothing else changes. But this assumption rarely holds since development is typically accompanied by shifts in the relative prices of child quantity and quality and a value change that emphasizes quality over quantity. Furthermore, social development also reduces the importance of child labor, and the opening of avenues for financial saving for old age and the provision of public social security schemes reduce the value of children as securing old age support for parents.

Changing direction of the flow of wealth

A variant of economic reasoning has been suggested by Caldwell (2005) in an effort to integrate economic with cultural and institutional reasons. In this view, the main driver behind the fertility transition lies in a change in the direction and magnitude of intergenerational wealth flows. Caldwell argued that in traditional settings the flow is typically from the children to the parents in terms of child labor: helping on the farm and, importantly, later in life providing economic support in parents' old age. With changing social and economic conditions this economic support of the younger generation for the older weakens and ultimately reverses. In modern urban societies children are increasingly an economic burden for their parents in terms of housing costs and education expenditures with very little returns expected later in life.

Caldwell identified female mass education as a key driver of fertility decline (Caldwell, 1980). But he assumed that the impact of education is not direct but through the restructuring of family relationships and, consequently, the change in direction of net wealth flows. He identified five mechanisms by which education impacts on fertility: (1) it reduces the child's potential contribution to the home economy through attending school; (2) education increases the cost of children beyond school fees, uniforms and other direct expenditure but also in raising the standards of what children demand from their parents; (3) schooling creates economic dependency in both family and society with the contribution of the child not being given at present but being expected for the future; (4) schooling speeds up cultural change and creates new cultures; and (5) the school serves as a major instrument for propagating the values of the Western middle class in developing countries. This list of five mechanisms gives an interesting blend of economic and cultural reasoning. Although Caldwell did not directly address the effect of education on cognition, three of these five reasons refer to a change in the way the world is perceived through education. And Caldwell (1980) concludes with an interesting observation which also has policy relevance by pointing out that the evidence suggests that the most potent force for change is the breadth of education (the proportion receiving some schooling) rather than the depth (length and quality of schooling for those who attend school). This is fully in line with the emphasis of the importance of universal literacy that will be presented in the following chapter.

Gender roles and maternal health

Most of the economic models discussed above see the household as one decision-making body without differentiating between men and women, who may have different interests in the process of choosing to have another child. There is evidence that the positive income effect in the neo-classical model, under which higher income results in a higher number of children, seems to be operating in predominantly patriarchal systems. This ranges from European rulers in medieval times to oil-rich Arab populations in the contemporary world. A study by Skirbekk (2008) collecting the broadest possible dataset on social status and fertility over the last few centuries shows that once the fertility decline has started, the relationship tends to turn negative and that for education it has always been negative. This seems to be particularly the case when one studies the role of education of women in a household as opposed to that of the men in the same household.

This already points to one of the main problems of economic analysis of fertility where the relevant agent is almost always assumed to be the household as a unit without differentiating the role and the interests of women from those of men. This may also have to do with the fact that economic data have been typically collected at the household level without differentiating between different members of the household. Meanwhile, in demography there is a large body of literature dealing with gender equity in relation to fertility. McDonald (2000) distinguishes between gender equity within the family and gender equity in society. He argues that there is a strong case that, where women are provided with decision-making power within the family, especially in regard to the number of children that they have, it is possible that fertility can fall to low levels without there being major changes in women's lives outside of the family. Fertility in the West fell to replacement level by the 1930s at the same time as the male breadwinner model was more dominant than ever before. He thus points at the fact that fertility can fall to low levels while most institutions outside the family may still have high gender inequality. And there is little doubt that increasing levels of female education relative to men have been a major driver for strengthening the position of women within families.

Once women have more decision-making power within families, health concerns also figure prominently. Having many pregnancies at short intervals comes with high health burden and health risks, particularly under conditions of poorly developed healthcare systems. Many studies have shown the key importance of female education on maternal health. Weitzman (2017), using causal analysis based on a natural experiment in Peru, shows that extending women's years of schooling strongly reduced the probability of several maternal health complications at last pregnancy/ birth. This seems to operate through various mechanisms, including the probability of short birth intervals and unplanned pregnancies (which may result in unsafe abortions) and to increase antenatal healthcare use, potentially owing to changes in women's cognitive skills, economic resources, and autonomy. There is also clear evidence that better edu- cated women find better access to reproductive health services and show a higher prevalence of contraceptive use (Lutz, 2014a).

Contraception and girls' education bringing down high fertility

Over the past few decades there has been a fierce debate about the role of family planning programs in helping to bring down fertility in countries that are still in the early stages of their fertility transition. The empirical evidence is difficult to assess because, in many countries that showed strong fertility declines, typically several potential drivers changed at the same time. In particular, some of the countries in East and Southeast Asia had effective family planning programs in parallel with a rapid expansion in the education of reproductive-age women.

There is little doubt that improving the education of girls more or less directly translates into lower fertility through a combination of lower desired family size, better empowerment of women to pursue their own plans and better ways of finding access to effective contraception. There is massive empirical evidence supporting this view, which has been reviewed in Lutz and KC (2011) and Lutz et al. (2014). This evidence is also suc- cinctly summarized in a paper by Bongaarts (2010) entitled "The causes of educational differences in fertility in Sub-Saharan Africa" in which he shows for 30 countries using DHS data that not only is desired family size significantly lower for more educated women but also that "as education rises, fertility is lower at a given level of contraceptive use, contraceptive use is higher at a given level of demand, and demand is higher at a given level of desired family size" (Bongaarts, 2010, p. 31). To illustrate this pervasive relationship between female education and contraceptive use, Figure 3.2 shows the pattern for DHS countries in West Africa – the world region that still has the highest level of fertility.

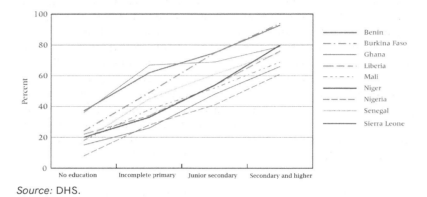

Source: DHS.

Figure 3.2   Ever-use of contraception by educational attainment of women. DHS data for nine countries in West Africa

But not all women who say that they want no more births are actually using modern contraception. This observation has given rise to the development of the concept of "meeting the unmet need", which has been defined as the number of women at risk of unwanted pregnancy who are not practicing modern contraception. This notion of defining an unmet need seemed to be the magic bullet that helped to consolidate the concern of the International Conference for Population and Development (ICPD, Cairo 1994) for individual rights while respecting individually desired family size with the still tacitly underlying pre-Cairo aggregate-level goal of bringing down fertility levels in high fertility countries. This concept has even risen to the highest level of international development policy prominence by being included as one of the six indicators used for Goal 5 (maternal and reproductive health) of the Millennium Development Goals (MDGs 2000). In the Sustainable Development Goals (SDGs 2015) the notion is not explicitly used but Target 3.7 calls on countries "by 2030, to ensure universal access to sexual and reproductive health-care services, including for family planning, information and education, and the integration of reproductive health into national strategies and programmes".

To this day, the concept of unmet need is still widely considered a valuable concept which is frequently used for advocacy of reproductive health and family planning programs. Sometimes quantitative information on the prevalence of unmet need in developing countries is presented together with some hypothetical calculations showing how much lower fertility levels in those countries would be in case the unmet need was met (Bradley et al., 2012). This is based on the strong assumption that somehow programs that improve the supply of contraceptives and lower their cost would lead to a near elimination of the unmet need. Lutz (2014a) presents empirical evidence that casts strong doubts on this assumption, and shows that investments in girls' education are likely to be a more efficient strategy towards lower fertility because education also decreases desired family size and can better help to remove some key obstacles to meeting the unmet need than a focus on the provision of supply of contraceptives. One can distinguish between the unmet need for spacing and the unmet need for limiting. Only the latter could meaningfully be related to estimates of how many births could be avoided in the case that the unmet need could be fulfilled.

A large number of recent DHS surveys included a specific set of questions asking women who had been classified as having an unmet need what were the obstacles or reasons for not using contraception. An analysis of these data shows that the two dominating reasons were fear of negative health effects and lack of exposure. For uneducated women, opposition to family planning (mostly by the partner or extended family) was an even more frequently cited reason than lack of exposure (Lutz, 2014a). The most surprising and politically relevant aspect of this analysis is the fact that the obstacles that are most directly addressed by family planning services, such as access to contraception and cost of contraception, seem to be of only minor importance. This has also been shown by other studies of the data on obstacles to contraception (Bradley et al., 2012). The DHS data show that of all African women who are classified as having an unmet need for contraception less than 3 percent cite lack of access as an important reason for not using contraception. Among more-educated women this percentage lies below 1 percent. Others cite the high cost of contraceptives as an obstacle, but overall, for uneducated African women who are classified as having an unmet need for contraception, only 8.5 percent say that either lack of access or high costs are an important reason and for women with secondary education only 3.3 percent mention these reasons. This seems to indicate that simply providing easier access will not lead to major declines in fertility. But to the extent that family planning programs also include counseling and education elements – as many of the programs on the ground do – they are likely to also address some of the other obstacles mentioned. However, even if programs are successful in reducing these other obstacles, the net effect of fertility would still be much smaller than the likely education effects that also address desired family size.

Consistent patterns of fertility differentials by mothers' education have been found from medieval times to the present in virtually all countries and at very different stages of economic developments (Skirbekk, 2008). The differentials are particularly pronounced when countries are still in the midst of the process of demographic transition (Fuchs & Goujon, 2014). The empirical evidence for a strong fertility-reducing effect of education in today's high and medium fertility countries is overwhelming, although there are some country-specific peculiarities in terms of average levels. But in virtually all developing countries there is a clear ranking within the countries where women who never went to school consistently have the highest fertility levels, and with each category of more education fertility levels are lower. Among all continents, the highest fertility levels today are in Africa where studies on the causes of educational fertility differentials consistently show that better-educated women want fewer children, have greater autonomy in reproductive decision-making, more knowledge about and access to contraception, and are more motivated to practice family planning (Bongaarts, 2010). Only in recent years in the Nordic countries does the gradient seem to flatten or show a mild U-shape because better-educated women can arrange their lives in a way to actually achieve the two-child norm, which is currently almost universal in Europe (Sobotka & Beaujouan, 2014).

Viewing the relationship between female education and fertility in more general terms, the empowering effect of education enables women in high fertility settings to want fewer children and find effective ways to have fewer children. As discussed above, they generally want fewer children for health reasons, as many births at short intervals can be a major risk in the absence of effective health services, and – because of value change – preferring fewer children who each will have better life chances, and possibly also because of higher opportunity costs. In addition, better-educated women can better resist the traditional pro-natalist norms in their societies and resist the often higher fertility desires of their husbands (Lutz, 2014a).

This strong emphasis of the role of girls' education is not to say that investments in female education should be played against investments in reproductive health services. In fact, there are good reasons to assume that both are strongly synergistic and strong female education programs combined with high quality reproductive health programs are the best way to go. This close interaction between comprehensive family planning efforts and female education in determining contraceptive prevalence has just been confirmed by a recent study by Bongaarts and Hardee (2019). In particular, strong public support for the concept of conscious family limitation together with the empowerment of women to be more equal with their husbands in matters of family-level decision-making is likely to lead to lowering both desired family size and the unmet need for contraception, jointly resulting in fertility decline from initially high levels.

How these pervasive education differentials in fertility levels can be incorporated into multi-dimensional models of population dynamics will be discussed in more detail in the context of the SSP scenarios in Chapter 4. Here, I just want to point at an earlier study that used the exact same assumed future fertility trajectories by level of education and only changed the assumptions concerning future education expansion (Lutz & KC, 2011). A quantification of this pure education effect has shown – based on 2000 data – that assuming constant school enrollment results in a world population size by 2050 that is one billion higher than in the case of assuming a very rapid education expansion, as has been experienced in Singapore or South Korea over the second half of the 20th century. This is yet another example of how the multi-dimensional perspective incorporating education yields a very different view of the future.

Stalled fertility declines in Africa

The future pace of fertility decline in Sub-Saharan Africa will likely be the chief determinant of future world population growth, with massive implications for Africa itself as well as the rest of the world. Sub-Saharan Africa stands out as the world's last region to progress in, or even enter, the fertility transition. It was only in the 1980s that birth rates started to fall in most Sub-Saharan African countries, and still these declines have been uneven and have stalled at times. Particularly in the late 1990s and early

2000s, many of these countries experienced a slowdown of their fertility decline and, in some cases, even a reversal, the reasons for which have remained largely unexplained (Kebede et al., 2019). Most existing studies try to link stalls in fertility decline to some specific contemporary factors, such as slower socio-economic development (Shapiro & Gebreselassie, 2008), the low priority assigned to family planning programs at the beginning of the 21st century (Bongaarts, 2008) and other factors related to public and reproductive health.

A very different perspective on this phenomenon has been offered by Goujon, Lutz and KC (2015) who proposed another plausible explanation focusing on cohort effects. They linked the fertility stalls around 2000 to the fact that some cohorts of women were subjected to an education stall, possibly associated with post-independence economic and political turmoil as well as structural adjustment over the 1980s. To explore this hypothesis, another recent study by Kebede et al. (2019) combined individual level data from Demographic and Health Surveys for 18 African countries – with and without fertility stalls – thus creating a pooled dataset of more than 2 million births to some 670,000 women born between 1950 and 1995 by level of education. The results showed that disruptions in the improvement of educational attainment among cohorts born around 1980 are consistent with populations having higher proportions of poorly educated women of childbearing ages in the late 1990s and early 2000s, than would otherwise have been the case had educational improvements continued to progress. This phenomenon, coupled with the relatively higher vulnerability of less-educated women to period effects, has likely contributed to stalls in the period fertility declines (Kebede et al., 2019).

To assess the effect of these two different forces being combined, the study compared actual fertility trends with a counterfactual, i.e., a hypothetical, scenario of what would have happened without this educational stall. The difference between the counterfactual TFRs assuming no earlier stall in education and the observed ones lies only in the weights given to the three educational groups (no formal education, incomplete primary, and completed primary education or more).

The simulation results (see Figure 3.3) show a sizable difference between the actual and counterfactual TFR around the year 2000 in the stalled-fertility countries. In absolute numbers for all ten stalled-fertility countries, between 1995 and 2010, this translates into about 13 million

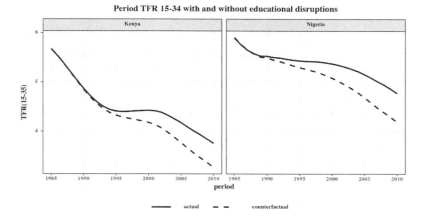

Period TFR 15-34 with and without educational disruptions

Source: Kebede et al. (2019).

Figure 3.3   Actual and simulated counterfactual fertility trends
in Kenya and Nigeria illustrating the impact of an
education stall in the 1980s on a fertility stall around
2000 (the counterfactual is based on the assumption of
no education stall)

fewer births to women aged 15–34. For Nigeria alone, the difference is
about 6.5 million births.

This study also highlights the importance of being aware of cohort effects
as described under the theory of Demographic Metabolism in Chapter 2.
The delayed consequences of educational disruptions on fertility levels
two decades later have gone largely unnoticed in the scientific literature
about Sub-Saharan Africa. An under-appreciation of this connection
– between girls' education and fertility in the following years – could
have serious implications for the societies in question, as they attempt to
maintain their living standards amid growing demands from prolonged
rapid population increases.

What will determine fertility levels at the end of demographic transition?[3]

The long-term trends of fertility in different parts of the world will directly influence the future number of humans living on our planet and thus greatly matter for sustainable development and future human well-being. Progress in the global demographic transition and the resulting changes in the size and structures of human populations have been shown to be a key driver of modern economic growth through several mechanisms and have been identified as an important factor in influencing climate change and other environmental factors (Bongaarts & O'Neill, 2018). So far, we have focused on the speed of fertility decline and its determinants in current high fertility populations as a determinant of future population size. Here we will discuss the question of how low can fertility fall and what is likely to be its long-term level after the demographic transition. In the very long run this level will be the key determinant of global population size.

Lutz (2020) argues that the key determinant of long-term fertility lies in changes in ideal family size – which here will be used synonymously with desired family size – and that these are primarily changes that happen in our minds and that are only in a secondary way influenced by changing economic realities and environmental factors. I also prefer to use the notion of ideal family size because it directly links to the notion of developmental idealism that has been introduced with respect to family norms by Arland Thornton (2005). This approach is based on the premise that our actions are a consequence of our norms and what we consider as good and desirable in our minds. However, in order to realize these desires we need to be empowered to do so. This empowerment has several dimensions that go from women being able to convince their partners – and in some societies also the extended family and peers – to allow them to pursue their family size desires, to having access to acceptable means of contraception and reproductive health services (including medically assisted reproduction). As is argued throughout this volume, for many of the dimensions of this reproductive empowerment female education is a decisive factor.

Unlike in the above-discussed high-fertility countries where the factors leading to fertility decline are relatively clear and the only open question is the exact timing of this decline, the main drivers and long-term trends are much more uncertain in populations that have reached the end of the demographic transition. Here we are groping in the dark and only feel confident to say that the long-held view that ultimately all countries will converge to the so-called replacement level of 2.1 is untenable and without scientific founding. As will be discussed in the next chapter, it had been the result of some sort of homeostasis thinking, which assumes that there is an inherent tendency of populations to reach a state of equilibrium in which they neither grow nor decline. This view has also been reinforced by the ubiquity of the United Nations population projections that for decades had assumed that life expectancy would level off at a certain level – which had to be shifted up and up as reality surpassed the assumptions – and fertility levels would all converge to replacement, thus reaching eternal stability after some turmoil caused by the demographic regime changes associated with the demographic transition. This view was also politically convenient for the United Nations because it told governments that everything will stabilize, and their populations would neither explode nor shrink and ultimately disappear. Unfortunately, reality has turned out to be different and today an increasing number of governments – mostly in Eastern Europe – are deeply concerned about depopulation, not only due to low fertility but also out-migration.

In global population projections, the long-term target fertility has now been lowered from 2.1 to somewhere between 1.75 and 1.85 (Lutz, Butz, et al., 2014; United Nations, 2019) but there is no convincing scientific rationale for choosing such assumed numbers. Hence, one may ask why then such long-term projections are even produced. The problem is that long-term population projections are needed for many purposes – e.g., the study of climate change and the human populations affected in different parts of the world – and for doing such projections one must assume some TFRs for the long run even if the scientific basis for doing so is very tenuous. Gietel-Basten et al. (2013) have presented some sensitivity analyses as to what would be the very long-term implications of different ultimate fertility levels. In the scenarios that assume a maximum life expectancy at birth of 100 years and that the stated fertility levels will be reached in all parts of the world by 2050, a long-term TFR of 1.75 would result in a world population of 8.5 billion in 2100, 5.6 billion in 2200 and 3.2 billion in 2300. Should the TFRs converge to 2.0 by 2050 the long-term population size would be in the 10–11 billion range over the coming centuries. If the TFR converges to 1.5 – which is around the current European average – the world population would – after peaking at 8.6 billion –

decline to 6.9 billion by 2100 and further to 2.7 billion in 2200 and 0.9 billion in 2300. In other words, the current European levels, which are still higher than the levels currently observed in East Asia, would in the very long run bring the world population down to below 1 billion, a size that humanity has seen throughout its entire history up until around 1800.

These purely hypothetical scenario calculations show that minor differences in fertility levels can have massive consequences for long-term population size. And my point here is that the question of average fertility being 1.50 or rather 1.75 or 2.00 will primarily depend on the ideal that will be in the minds of people as to what is a desirable number of children for a successful and happy life. This view has been embedded in the so-called "Low Fertility Trap Hypothesis (LFTH)" (Lutz, Skirbekk, et al., 2006). It assumes the following hierarchy affecting fertility and births: personal ideal family size is the fundamental driver of fertility, which is then transformed into a specific family size target when conflicting interests and constraints are taken into account. In a next step, these fertility targets are translated into period fertility rates that are sensitive to choices around the timing of births. Finally, period fertility rates translate into certain absolute numbers of births in a given calendar year when the changing age structure of the population is also taken into consideration. At each of these steps external influences come into play, which partly represent feedbacks from earlier fertility levels, as is evident in the case of the age structure of the population and the number of young people entering the reproductive ages. But the key hypothesis of the LFTH is that the most basic underlying determinant, namely personal ideal family size, is in part determined by what young people have been socialized into and what they see as the new norm pursued by other people around them. These experiences shape their own norms about family size. This can also be seen as a feedback from earlier declines in fertility, resulting in lower actual family sizes in society, which in turn influence the family size norms of the next generation. This mechanism by itself could result in a downward spiral of ever lower fertility ideals and ever lower actual family size, if no other factors come into play.

In 2008, in a paper discussing the LFTH in Europe and East Asia I asked "Has Korea's fertility reached the bottom?" (Lutz, 2008). At that time the TFR in South Korea was 1.25 and few people believed it could fall even lower. In 2018 and 2019 the Korean TFR has actually fallen below 1.0. Part of this very low period fertility level is likely due to tempo effects which are a consequence of postponement of births. But the extent fertility will recover over the coming years is not clear at all. Following the LFTH framework, this very low level could also be due to a change in either the ideal family size or important competing aspirations and conflicts resulting in lower target fertility or a combination of both. There is not yet enough empirical evidence to disentangle these different determinants of fertility in East Asia. However, in the urban areas of China there is some evidence that after many years of a one-child policy and a situation where indeed most couples do actually have only one child, this has become the new norm and a large majority of couples do indeed want only one child even though they are now allowed to have two (Basten & Jiang, 2015).

In Europe, in contrast, the two-child norm still seems to be dominant, at least until recently (Sobotka & Beaujouan, 2014). Over the last decade several European countries have shown a rather unexpected decline in fertility rates, which is particularly puzzling for the Nordic countries that used to be the prime example for the view that good compatibility between work and family and generous child support systems do result in relatively high fertility levels. In Norway, for example the TFR has declined from 1.96 in 2008 to 1.56 in 2018. In Finland it has declined from 1.85 to 1.40 over the same time without any clearly identifiable social, economic or family policy changes happening. Demography is still groping in the dark in terms of explaining these changes. But there may well have been some ongoing cultural changes affecting the relative importance of children and, in consequence, ideal family size.

Will the empowerment of women as enhanced by education – a main factor in bringing down high fertility – also matter for the future level of fertility in low fertility settings? I have argued elsewhere (Lutz, 2017a) that it can help to explain an emerging U-shape in the relationship between education and fertility in some socially advanced low fertility countries such as Sweden. Assume for the time being that ideal family size is two children for all women irrespective of education. Then for women with low education there will be a relatively higher level of fertility because there is still a degree of fatalism in their reproductive behavior and a higher proportion of unplanned births can be expected. At the other extreme, women with high education tend to be able to plan their lives more effectively, although they do often have to deal with difficult trade-offs in terms of advancing their careers and establishing a family. However, they also tend to have higher human and social capital to better combine work and family life and therefore will be able to come closer to their ideal family size, which in Europe still tends to be two children. Women with intermediate levels of education and associated job may have a harder time to reach their ideal family size and end up with slightly lower fertility.

We may also ask whether there is something in our genes that will assure a certain minimal level of fertility. From a purely biological perspective, the sex drive seems to be the main mechanism that evolution produced for assuring that there will be sufficient reproduction. This is also reflected in Robert Malthus' famous statement that fertility is unlikely to decline because "the passion between the sexes will never diminish" (Malthus, 1798). But, thanks to contraception, fertility around the world has declined even with the passion not diminishing. Reproduction has now mostly entered the realm of conscious choice (Coale, 1973). And where will this conscious choice lead us? I got the clearest but still somewhat unsatisfactory answer to these crucial questions from one of the leading evolutionary biologists, Simon Levin of Princeton. To my question as to whether human evolution will assure a certain minimum level of reproduction, his short answer was "Once reproduction is culturally determined, cultural evolution can bring you almost anywhere". And the key mechanism through which culture works is via the shaping of ideal family size as the fundamental determinant of future fertility.

In a nutshell, the long-term future of the level of human fertility in different populations and in the world as a whole is indeterminate. There is reason to assume that – unlike in the natural sciences – it is not our incomplete understanding of the system that is the reason for this ignorance but rather that the system of human cultural evolution is intrinsically indeterminate and thus unpredictable in the long run. What is predictable, however, is the range of possible changes over the coming decades through the above-described slowly but surely evolving demographic metabolism. But uncertainty at the margins – in terms of the effects of different levels of fertility and mortality – increases over time and, for this reason, we have to operate with different scenarios for the longer-term future, which will be the topic of the next chapter.

Notes

1. This section is partly based on an unpublished text contributed by Harold Lentzner and Elsie Pamuk which I gratefully acknowledge.
2. The World Health Surveys (WHS) is a collection of sample surveys of the adult population of 18 years of age and older in 70 countries around the globe.
3. This section draws in part on Lutz (2020).

4 Demographic futures and sustainable development

To think about the demographic future, we first need to have information about the present. The total size of the world's population in 2021 – the year in which this volume has been finalized – is estimated at 7.8–7.9 billion people and is likely to hit the 8 billion mark over the following couple of years. I emphasize the word "estimated" because there is no exact total count of the people on this planet at any current point in time. The measurement mechanism that comes closest to resulting in a total count is the series of censuses taken regularly in almost every country, typically every 10 years. Since the publication of census results often takes several years, for the 2020/21 round of censuses no global level data are yet available. For this reason, the last available empirical information for most countries dates from the 2010/11 round of censuses and for some countries even from earlier times or other census years. For the year 2010, this latest mostly empirical information shows a total world population of still somewhat below 7.0 billion (United Nations, 2019). Actually, the United Nations had proclaimed one specific day, October 31, 2011, to be the "day of seven billion",[1] which was clearly an estimate based on projections with the last empirical basis mostly in the 2000/2001 round of censuses. For 2000, the world population was estimated around 6.1 billion. Thus, over the course of the 20th century the world population increased from 1.6 to 6.1 billion – numbers easy to remember.

Since population forecasting has recently become a rather controversial topic with differences between alternative projections being discussed not only in the scientific literature but also in popular media, we will start this chapter with a brief overview of different approaches to population forecasting and how the choice of approach can influence the resulting projections. In the two following sections we will discuss the application of demographic forecasting models to the two areas of application that are most hotly debated in terms of their policy implications: the role of different future migration scenarios to the anticipated burden of aging in low fertility countries, and the role of alternative world population and human capital scenarios in the context of future global development, climate change and sustainable human well-being on this planet. Both applications show how demography can contribute to some of the hottest policy discussions of our times. The concerns range from the fear of depopulation in the Eastern part of Europe to fears about changing ethnic and religious composition in major Western countries, and fears about vulnerability to global environmental change in some of the poorest countries in Africa.

These two sections will also illustrate the use of two different methodologies of multi-dimensional demographic forecasting: micro-simulation, which is based on simulating the future lives of millions of individuals that can have a large number of relevant characteristics attached to them, and macro-simulation, or multi-dimensional cohort component projections with populations stratified by three dimensions, namely age, sex and level of educational attainment. In the final section, the lessons and implications of these projections will be pulled together and population policy priorities will be discussed.

Different approaches to population forecasting

There is no natural or self-evident way of doing population projections despite the fact that currently most demographers and statistical offices use a model that projects populations by age and sex using the so-called cohort component method with assumptions about future trends in fertility, mortality and migration applied to a given starting population by age and sex. But through most of demographic history, projections were simply carried out by applying an assumed growth rate to total population size without explicitly considering age structure. More recently, there have also been multi-dimensional cohort-component models as well as micro-simulation models that explicitly consider population heterogeneity beyond the conventional age and sex.

It is important to note that the nature of the model used significantly influences the outcomes of the projections in addition to the specific assumptions made. There have been different ways of coming up with assumptions about future fertility, mortality and migration trends ranging from trend extrapolations to expert-argument-based assumptions and various combinations of these approaches. Needless to say, different assumptions, e.g. about the future course of fertility, result in different projection results. And finally, there are different possible ways of dealing with uncertainty in population projections, ranging from ignoring uncertainty and only presenting one forecast, to providing scenarios that show the implications of alternative assumptions in one, more, or all of the components of change, to fully probabilistic population projections. In the following we summarize the implications of these different choices that have to be made when producing population forecasts.[2]

From simple growth rate to multi-dimensional models

The oldest known long-term world population projection was published in 1696 by British statistician Gregory King (1973), who projected the world population would reach 630 million in 1950 and 780 million in 2050. The method used by King, as well as by Pearl (1923, 1924) and Knibbs (1976) in the 1920s, was simple: combine an estimate of current world population size with assumed future rates of population growth. These early projections have been described by Frejka (1996), who states that the projections published by Pearl in 1924 gave a total world population of 1.96 billion for 2000 and a roughly constant population of 2 billion for 2050 and 2100. Knibbs' projections published only four years later, in 1928, assumed a higher growth rate that resulted in a projection of 3.9 billion in 2000. Evidently, these early projections have been far off the mark, with world population actually reaching 6.1 billion in 2000, because they assumed growth rates that were lower than those actually observed. And there is reason to assume that this poor performance is not due to the simple model used but rather to wrong assumptions made on the future course of the only parameter in the model. The first global cohort-component projection made by Notestein in 1944 used a much more elaborate model with age structure and separate assumptions for future fertility, mortality and migration and projected world population in 2000 of only 3.3 billion, mostly because his mortality assumptions were far too pessimistic (Notestein, 1944).

The cohort-component model by age and sex – which has been described formally in Chapter 1 – was proposed in the 19th century but was only gradually replacing the simple growth rate model by the middle of the 20th century, presumably because the age distributions of many European populations had become very irregular as a consequence of the First World War and the subsequent very low fertility rates. As long as the age pyramid is smooth and regular and does not change much over time there is not much difference between the results of the simple growth rate model and the much more elaborate cohort-component model, which needs to make assumptions on a much larger number of parameters, such as sets of age-specific fertility rates and age- and sex-specific mortality and migration rates. Why should one choose a complicated model with many more necessary assumptions to be made if the simple model can also do the job? This is also the reason why, in the field of wildlife and animal demography up to today, the simple growth rate models are the standard (Sibly et al., 2003). This question of whether it is better to always have a fully age-structured model compared with a simple growth rate model has led to some more general debates in demography (see Rogers, 1995) that were recently picked up again in the context of the discussion of whether three-dimensional models (considering age, sex and level of education) are always preferable to the conventional two-dimensional models (considering only age and sex) (KC et al., 2018).

In this discussion, we have to distinguish between two quite different questions: (1) which are the output variables that one is interested in, and (2) how does explicit accounting for population heterogeneity affect the aggregate results? If the interest is mainly in forecasting total population size, then an explicit incorporation of heterogeneity by age, sex or level of education is only to be judged with respect to the second question. If there is also interest in forecasts of the changing age structure of the population in its own right, e.g. for purposes of school planning or old-age care systems, then this is an important reason for explicitly including age structure in the model, and if there is interest in forecasting the future educational attainment distribution of the population by age and sex for economic analysis, health or many behavioral and institutional factors related to education, then this is a good reason for explicitly incorporating education in the model. The same is true, for example, for labor force participation or the future ethnic composition of the population. As argued in the introduction of this book, demographic forecasts of the future distributions of such relevant human characteristics in the population tend to make demography as a discipline much more relevant for the consideration of social, economic and even environmental problems than just projecting total population size. This alone is a weighty reason for carrying out multi-dimensional population projections.

As addressed by the second question, accounting for measurable heterogeneity within populations can also impact on the forecast of total population size at the aggregate level, if there are changes in the underlying population composition that matter for the outcome. An obvious example has been given above with respect to the highly irregular age distributions that appeared in European populations after the First World War. If in one country unusually small cohorts of women enter the prime childbearing ages, then the number of births in the subsequent years will be lower even if every woman has the same number of children. Hence, the resulting growth rate of the population will be lower than a simple aggregate level extrapolation of the past growth rates would suggest. This additional knowledge about discontinuities in the cohort size of women of reproductive age can clearly contribute to improving the accuracy of the forecast. Similarly, incorporating a discontinuity in the educational attainment distribution of women entering reproductive age can – given the effect of education on fertility – result in different fertility levels than an extrapolation of the past trend in total fertility would have suggested. In the previous chapter we illustrated this with the example of the stalled fertility decline in some African countries, which could be associated with an earlier stall in the education expansion trend in these countries. Hence, more generally, if there is a discontinuity in the change of the population composition with respect to a driver of demographic outcomes – such as female education for fertility – then explicitly accounting for this heterogeneity of the population makes the projection more accurate. Or, in other words, if this is the case then the forecast for total population size resulting from a model including age, sex and education will be more accurate than from a model only incorporating age and sex, even in a case where is no particular interest in the distribution of education in its own right.

It is important to note here that, in addition to these observable sources of population heterogeneity, there is still unobserved heterogeneity in every population which is hard to capture empirically. Theoretical considerations suggest that such unobserved heterogeneity can significantly impact future population dynamics (Vaupel & Yashin, 1985), but there is little one can do about it except to be aware of the problem and be cautious about the validity of the conclusions drawn. Given this problem associated with hidden heterogeneity, it is even more important to explicitly measure and incorporate the observable sources of population heterogeneity wherever feasible, and thus try to minimize the possible biases caused by overall heterogeneity (Lutz & KC, 2010).

Statistical extrapolation versus expert arguments and knowledge

"Can knowledge improve forecasts?" was the title of a famous paper by Nathan Keyfitz (1982), in which he expressed the view that demographic trends are easier to forecast than many social and economic trends, which are often seen as drivers of fertility and mortality. But on what basis should we forecast the demographic trends themselves? What should be the basis for assumptions about future fertility, mortality, and migration trends? Ahlburg and Lutz (1999), in the introduction to a special issue of *Population and Development Review* on the topic "Frontiers of Population Forecasting" (Lutz et al., 1999), interpret this view – after personal discussions with Nathan Keyfitz at IIASA about this topic – by suggesting that demographic trends should not be entirely derived from other forecasts as in the case of the fertility and mortality functions in the above discussed World 3 Model of the "Limits to Growth" by Meadows et al. (1972) nor should they be based on blind extrapolation or replication of past trends. Instead, they suggest summarizing the scientific community's knowledge base concerning future demographic trends through a structured process of expert solicitation. Focusing on consolidated and peer-reviewed experts' argument as the most science-based approach is a view that was also inspired by the influential work of Armstrong and colleagues on forecasting outside the realm of demography (Armstrong & Collopy, 1992). They clearly demonstrated that structured judgement outperforms either subjective judgement alone or a statistical model alone (Ahlburg & Lutz, 1999).

The practices in national statistical offices have for long been moving in this direction of using structured expert judgement for defining the assumptions. Virtually all national statistical agencies in the world, as well as inter-governmental agencies such as the United Nations (until recently) and Eurostat, have been producing regular population projections by age and sex, following the cohort-component projection method in which groups of experts have engaged in some science-based discussions when drawing up the assumptions on future fertility, mortality and migration. In 2005, all national statistical offices of the European Union countries were asked by Eurostat to provide information on their procedures for producing their most recent population projections. It turned out that the most common procedure was to create scenarios that cover a "plausible" range of future fertility, mortality, and migration trends. The involvement of external experts and meetings was generally considered very important and the majority of national statistical offices try to describe the reasoning behind the assumptions in their publications about the population projection (Lutz & Skirbekk, 2014). This suggested approach of not asking experts for their "opinions" about future trends but rather ask them to assess the validity of alternative possible arguments with respect to the drivers of future fertility, mortality and migration trends in their countries of expertise was systematically developed for a major global online inquiry in which over 550 population experts from around the world participated. The results are documented in Lutz, Butz and KC (2014) and translated into five alternative scenarios until 2100 for all countries in the world. These scenarios, following the narratives of the Shared Socioeconomic Pathways (SSPs), will be discussed later in this chapter.

The population projections which have been regularly published by the United Nations Population Division (UNPD) recently moved into a very different direction. For the second half of the 20th century up until the 2010 Assessment, their approach was to publish three variants – high, medium and low – which only differed by their fertility assumptions while using identical mortality and migration assumptions. By far the most frequently used variant was the medium variant, which was also considered to be the most likely future path with high and low variants simply assuming fertility trends that are 0.5 children higher and lower than the medium assumption. The fertility, mortality and migration assumptions for the medium variant for all countries of the world were entirely expert based until, in 2010, a completely new approach was introduced which bases assumptions largely on a Bayesian statistical model, using only past national level time series data and assuming essentially that the future course in each country follows that of other countries that are already more advanced in their demographic evolution (United Nations, 2019). This new United Nations approach is based on the belief that specific expert knowledge does not help and the future will see a replication of past trends interpreted within the framework of their statistical model. But in the model structure itself some expert judgements are hidden concerning the patterns of change and the assumed long-term levels of fertility, mortality and migration to which countries are heading. There is no room under this approach for country-specific expertise, for the consideration of substantive knowledge about the drivers of fertility, mortality and migration, or for possible feedbacks from reaching environmental or other constraints. For this reason, I have also called this a blind statistical extrapolation model. It is a highly sophisticated statistical model using state-of-the-art Bayesian methods, unlike some other extrapolative population projections that essentially apply a ruler to the trend of fertility and mortality rates. But it still leaves no room for substantive scientific reasoning.

Many people seem to hold the view that such a statistical extrapolation approach is the best one can do since the main problem with expert opinions is that they tend to be opinionated; this can result in undesirable biases and distortions that do not necessarily reflect the state of knowledge. There is indeed abundant evidence that experts tend to hold strong beliefs about the future that are at the level of emotions and intuitions (Lutz, 2009). For this reason, the approach applied in Lutz, Butz and KC (2014) goes far beyond opinion-based Delphi approaches and applies a more objective science-based procedure in which experts are asked to assess alternative arguments in terms of their validity and relevance in a peer-review type manner. But cognitive science tells us that at some point even such science-based assessments end up with some level of intuitive judgement which inevitably contains elements of subjectivity (Lutz & Skirbekk, 2014). The challenge is to design procedures in which, through inter-subjective argumentation, consensus finding where possible, and documentation of differences where there is no consensus, the role of subjectivity in judgement be will reduced substantially.

It is important to note that there never can be a purely objective way of data-based forecasting because data never speak for themselves. Data must always be interpreted in a context. This starts with choice of indicators that shall be assessed in their past trends and extrapolated into the future and with the choice of the dimensionality of the model (forecasting only population size or multi-dimensional structures) as discussed above. A particularly tricky problem in any model based on national time series data – such as the one currently used by the United Nations – is how to weigh the experiences of the past. While in economics it is standard practice to give every country equal weight when the variables studied are derived from national accounting, this approach may well be questioned when the variables studied are, for example, fertility trends that result from the decisions of individual couples rather than national governments. Should all past national level fertility data be given equal weight, irrespective of whether they summarize the experience of only a few thousand couples in a small country or hundreds of millions of couples in a big country? Because, in fertility, couples – not national governments – are the relevant decision-making units, and many countries are highly heterogeneous with respect to the conditions under which reproductive behavior takes place, one could well argue that couples rather than countries are the independent units of observation that should be given equal weight (Abel et al., 2016). Doing so would completely change the projection results of extrapolative statistical models such as the one used by the United Nations, which currently gives the experience of the five small Nordic countries with very similar welfare systems much more weight than the very heterogeneous experience of the more than one billion Indians.

There is no easy solution to this issue of expert judgement versus extrapolation of past trends. The best is probably a hybrid approach that tries to combine the best of both worlds with expert knowledge trying to assess the plausibility of extrapolated trends in specific settings. And it is most important that the approach chosen and the specific choices made are as transparent and well-documented as possible and that the results presented give explicit recognition of the uncertainty involved in the projections. This brings us to the next topic.

How to represent uncertainty in population forecasting?

Most users of population forecasts for all kinds of practical purposes, ranging from city planning to reforms of the pension system, are likely satisfied with one "best guess" forecast. There also is frequent reference to one "official" projection, which carries more weight by the fact of being produced by a government body. But a growing number of users also want to know how reliable such forecasts are and what is the chance that the actual trend will turn out to be very different from the forecast trend. There is also increasing interest among population forecasters to provide the users with a fair representation of different sources of uncertainty, which include uncertainty about the baseline data, model uncertainty and uncertainty in the future trends of the components of demographic change (Ahlburg & Lutz, 1999). Up until the 1990s the conventional way of dealing with trend uncertainty, which was practiced by the United Nations as well as most national statistical offices, was to produce three variants with the medium variant considered the most likely and the high and low variants assuming somewhat higher and lower fertility levels. While this variants approach seemed intuitively appealing to most users in defining a possible range of future population trends it was strongly criticized by statistical demographers for several undesirable properties. Ronald Lee (1999) called this approach "probabilistically inconsistent", in particular with respect to aggregating the national high and low variants to regional and global ones with the high–low range getting a different probabilistic meaning. But there are several other problems with this approach, including the fact that it only considers uncertainty in fertility and does not represent the consequences of possible future deviations from the assumed mortality and migration trends. And it is not specific in telling the user as to whether the inter-variant range is supposed to cover 95 percent or 50 percent or any other proportion of possible future population trajectories.

This increasing dissatisfaction with the conventional high–medium–low variants approach led to developments into two opposing directions: fully probabilistic projections and probability-free scenarios. The specification of fully probabilistic projection models was either based on time-series modeling approaches considering annual fluctuations or on specified probability ranges of piece-wise linear trends in the components of population change as defined by experts. There is no space here to cover this rather technical discussion as to what is the most appropriate way for producing probabilistic population forecasts. For interested readers there are special issues of PDR (Lutz et al., 1999) and of the *International Statistical Review* (Lutz & Goldstein, 2004) which comprehensively discuss these topics. The most recent contribution to the discussion has been a book by Mazzuco and Keilman (2020), *Developments in Demographic Forecasting*.

One interesting proposal made in this literature is the production of conditional probabilistic projections which addresses one of the most important shortcomings of probabilistic projections, namely that they cannot be related to certain policies. Typically, such probabilistic projections are presented like a law of nature that is a given and cannot be influenced. But some governments might well be interested to see what would be the consequences on future population size and structure in the case of, for example, strictly limiting immigration while at the same time not having specific policies influencing future fertility or mortality. While the most frequently used approach for such policy questions is scenario analysis, there also is the possibility for probabilistic projections to condition the resulting distributions on certain sub-ranges of one component, such as only very low migration assumptions (O'Neill, 2004; Sanderson et al., 2004). This approach holds promise in the context of currently produced probabilistic projections, such as by the United Nations.

The alternative strategy for addressing uncertainty in population projections is to produce sets of scenarios that either systematically vary all the key parameters in a mechanistic way (such as combining high, medium or low fertility with high, medium or low mortality and migration) or to integrate the scenarios into broader narratives that draw consistent and comprehensive pictures of future developments. Such narratives go far beyond the field of demography and also include economic, social and even political and environmental changes. The currently most widely used set of such broad narratives was developed in the context of climate change analysis by the global integrated assessment modeling community in the form of the Shared Socioeconomic Pathways (SSPs), which have as their "human core" multi-dimensional population scenarios by age, sex and level of educational attainment for all countries in the world up to 2100, as will be discussed in the following section.

Population scenarios by level of education

Projections of future population size and structures are needed for a wide range of policy questions as well as commercial and private planning. They also matter at different levels of aggregation from the local to the regional, national and global level. There is also an interesting interaction between what demographers offer in terms of detail of information and what users expect. The long tradition of producing projections by age and sex for all countries has led to the expectation on the side of users, including experts in other fields, that this is the best that can be expected from demographers. A good example for this is the influential Working Group on Ageing in the European Commission, which has been charged by the finance ministers of all EU member countries to assess the fiscal and other economic implications of likely future demographic trends. Since they do not expect demographic projections to be able to contribute forecasts by relevant demographic characteristics other than age and sex, they have asked for scenarios on future labor force participation or productivity/education from economists that could not offer the important details by age, sex and patterns of cohort change that multi-dimensional demographic models can provide. This shows that the potentials of multi-dimensional demography are not yet widely enough known and appreciated. Later we will show what they have to offer in this respect for Europe.

In the next subsection we take a global perspective and address another important community of users of demographic forecasts, namely the global sustainable development research community and, more specifically, the community using integrated assessment models to study policies of climate change mitigation and adaptation. We will do this in the context of the so-called Shared Socioeconomic Pathways (SSPs) that are comprehensive scenarios based on alternative narratives in the field of future climate change and of which a recent set of three-dimensional demographic scenarios by age, sex and level of educational attainment for all countries of the world form the "human core". After addressing some global level results with a focus on the hotly discussed question of the end of world population growth, I will also illustrate the use of this extensive set of scenario results (as offered in the Wittgenstein Centre Data Explorer) for the assessment of future scenarios for one big developing country in Africa, Ethiopia, which in demographic and other development terms currently stands at the crossroads.

The end of world population growth with increasing human capital

"The end of world population growth in the 21st century: New challenges for human capital formation and sustainable development" also was the title of a 2004 book explaining in more detail this notion that had already been introduced in earlier articles (Lutz et al., 2001, 2004). Based on empirical information up to the late 1990s these expert-argument based probabilistic projections showed that there was a high chance, estimated at over two thirds, that world population would peak and then start to decline over the course of the 21st century. This assessment was qualitatively not so different from the United Nations medium projections which were published around the same time and which, in their medium variant, also saw a leveling off in world population growth over the last decades of the century.

Subsequently, two developments let to some upward correction in the projected world population growth. (1) A widely discussed unexpected stall in the fertility declines of some important African countries was observed where, around 2000–2005, fertility rates interrupted their earlier declines or even increased somewhat, as discussed in the previous chapter, which was likely the result of an earlier education stall. (2) Less widely discussed in this context is the great success of international health intervention efforts in significantly lowering child mortality rates in many African countries. While highly desirable in its own end this unexpectedly dramatic improvement in child survival also had the consequence of boosting population growth through more children staying alive and reaching reproductive age and having children themselves. These two factors in combination have led to the fact that today the world population outlook is somewhat higher than 15–20 years ago, but we still expect a global peak population to be reached during this century.

The long-term global population outlook matters decisively for the assessment of climate change and its implications. For more than a dozen years the Intergovernmental Panel on Climate Change (IPCC) modeling community had used the so-called SRES scenarios (Nakicenovic et al., 2000), which were very detailed on the energy, technology, and emissions side, but included only total population size as a demographic indicator. Thus, population essentially served as a scaling variable with no interactions between the demographic trajectories and other parts of the comprehensive scenario narratives. The subsequent Shared Socioeconomic Pathways (SSPs) are much more elaborate on the demographic side, including in each scenario and for every country the full age-, sex- and education-distributions of the population. The SSPs have five different narratives about the future that were defined with respect to different levels of socio-economic challenges to climate change mitigation (reducing greenhouse gas emissions where the challenges for a largely fossil-fuel based economy are greater than for one using lots of renewables) and adaptation (ability to reduce harm caused by a given degree of climate change). Since there is no space here to summarize the extensive literature on the SSPs, for the analysis presented in this section it suffices to point at three scenarios that greatly differ in their demographic assumptions: SSP1 is called "rapid social development" associated with rapid expansion of education, low mortality and rapid fertility decline in high fertility countries, SSP2 is called "middle of the road", and the other end SSP3 is called "stalled development" and is associated with very slow further progress in education, slow fertility decline and high mortality. The results of these alternative scenarios along the SSP narratives are fully documented for all countries as well as country groupings and continents in 5-year time steps and for 5-year age groups by sex, and six education levels in the Wittgenstein Centre Data Explorer (WIC, 2018).

The SSP3 scenario assumes stalled socio-economic development and thus has lower female education and higher fertility rates for each education group. It reaches the 10 billion mark around 2045 and then continues to grow over the rest of the century, reaching 13.4 billion in 2100. According to the narrative underlying this scenario this will be a very unpleasant future in which the world will be strongly fragmented, there will be widespread poverty, mortality will be rather high and the adaptive capacity to already unavoidable climate change will be very weak. This pretty much resembles a Malthusian scenario as described in Chapter 2.

In the SSP1 scenario, very rapid social and economic development leads to markedly lower population growth resulting in a peak population of around 8.9 billion in 2055–2060 followed by a decline to 7.8 billion by the end of the century. These 7.8 billion are actually exactly the population estimates for today (2021). In terms of the underlying narrative this scenario resembles a global development under which the sustainable development goals are met in most countries and significant progress in education and poverty reduction is made. As has been shown elsewhere (Abel et al., 2016) meeting SDG4 (on education) and SDG3 (on health including reproductive health) will be key factors in reducing global population growth.

The SSP2 scenario, finally, may be considered as bringing together assumptions that look most likely from today's perspective. In this middle-of-the-road scenario, world population reaches 9.4 billion in 2050, then peaks at 9.7 billion in 2070–2075 before starting a moderate decline to 9.3 billion in 2100.

In all scenarios, the world population will see a significant increase in the proportion of the population above age 65 as a combined consequence of low fertility rates and increasing life expectancy. In the middle-of-the-road (SSP2) scenario, the proportion above age 65 increases from currently 8.3 percent to 17 percent by mid-century and 29 percent by the end of the century. Under the rapid social development scenario (SSP1), which assumes faster increases in life expectancy combined with lower fertility, this proportion above age 65 even reaches around 20 percent in mid-century and 43 percent in 2100. The stalled development scenario (SSP3) on the other hand will see a much slower increase, reaching only 16 percent above age 65 by the end of the century.

Figure 4.1 plots the changes of the educational attainment distribution of the world population according to the two opposing scenarios SSP1 and SSP3. The projected trends in the middle-of-the-road scenario SSP2 have already been shown in Figure 1.5 in Chapter 1 and are hence not repeated here. In 2015, 14.0 percent of the world population above age 15 had no formal education at all and 14.7 percent had some sort of post-secondary education, making the global education distribution rather symmetric in its tails. Fifty percent of the adult population had some secondary (23 percent lower and 27 percent upper secondary) education. This already indicates a huge improvement in overall education levels given that, in 1950, almost half (46 percent) of the world population had never been to school, which declined to a third by 1970. At the other extreme, in 1950 only less than 2 percent of the adult world population had some post-secondary education, which increased to 4 percent by 1970.

In the middle-of-the-road (SSP2) scenario, continued significant progress will occur, with the proportion without any education declining to 5 percent by mid-century and being only 1 percent by 2100. Over the same time horizon, the proportion with post-secondary education increases to 38 percent in this scenario, which can be considered as most likely from today's perspective. Under the rapid development (SSP1) scenario, the proportion with post-secondary education increases to 32 percent in 2050 and 65 percent in 2100. These are, by any standard, stunning increases in the education and thus the human capital of the world.

However, further long-term progress in education is not guaranteed, despite the fact that today, in virtually all countries, the young generations are better educated than the older ones. In case that progress stalls, in the SSP3 scenario the combination of high population growth with little further schooling expansion can result in an increase of the proportion without any formal education by the end of the century. Because of the slow process of demographic metabolism as explained in Chapter 2, this reversal in trends is rather slow, but once it happens it will also develop momentum in the direction of a less educated and more divided world. While the countries in today's developed world and the emerging economies where the young generations are already fairly well educated might continue to enjoy high levels of education, the African and South Asian populations that have made less progress so far may actually become less educated because school expansion will not be able to keep pace with rapid population growth. We will now illustrate this for the case of Africa's second most populous country.

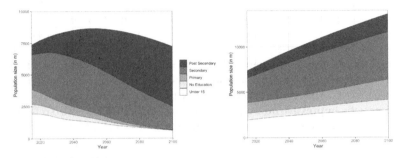

Source: WIC (2018).

Figure 4.1   World population by level of educational attainment 2015–2100. SSP1 scenario (left) and SSP3 scenario (right)

Ethiopia at the crossroads

In 1970, Ethiopia was a feudal country with 29 million inhabitants in which a small elite dominated an army of poor farmers. Haile Selassie was Emperor of Ethiopia from 1930 to 1974. In 1970 nearly half of all Ethiopians were under 16 years old, which reflected the high fertility rate of about seven children per woman, but also the fact that an average life lasted just 43 years. Hardly any adult woman had ever been to school. As seen from the age and education pyramid in Figure 4.2, among the youngest cohorts aged 15 to 19 only about 5 percent had some primary education. Young men at the time were already a bit better educated than women.

Given the extremely low level of education, the inefficiency of the government and the political situation, it is not surprising that Ethiopia remained an extremely poor country for a long time and became a symbol of Africa's failure. In addition to devastating droughts under the socialist dictatorship after the fall of Haile Selassie, Ethiopia underwent many years of ethnic conflicts, and was plagued by border disputes with neighbors. By 2010, that is within 40 years, the population had risen to 83 million and had therefore almost tripled. The annual per capita income, however, had only just reached the equivalent of US$350. The average Ethiopian had less than one dollar a day and the country was still one of the poorest in the world. But as the right pyramid in Figure 4.2 shows, despite the extreme poverty, school enrollment increased substantially. Although the number of young people had increased dramatically, the majority of them, both men and women, at least attended primary school, a certain percentage had a secondary school education and a few percent even went to university. As compared with other very poor countries, it is especially impressive how quickly women caught up. This is also reflected in the fertility rate, which declined from around 7.5 children per woman to currently around 4.0. But within the country there are still huge fertility differences by level of education. While the lowest education groups have around five children, women with completed secondary education have under two.

What do the SSP scenarios imply for the future of Ethiopia? First, the great momentum of demographic metabolism will lead to further improvements in adult educational attainment over the coming decades because the younger generations are already much better educated than the older ones. If the education boom of recent years continues, the outlook for the future will improve significantly. But if the school expansion stalls and is outpaced by the still rapid population growth, then this positive momentum can vanish over the coming decades and, because of the still relatively high fertility rates, there is no guarantee that this trend will continue.

This is exactly what the two scenarios for Ethiopia show (Figure 4.3). In the best case, by 2030 all children will have the opportunity to attend school and a growing number of young people will attend a secondary school

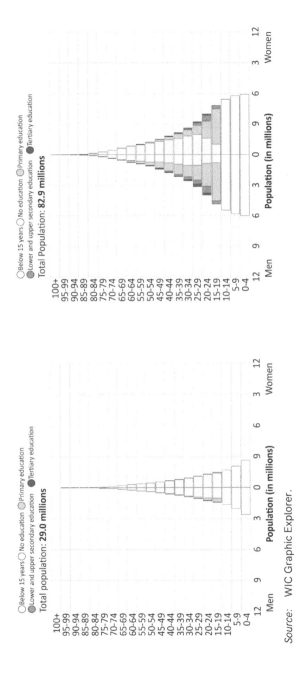

Source: WIC Graphic Explorer.

Figure 4.2   Age and education pyramid for Ethiopia in 1970 (left) and 2010 (right)

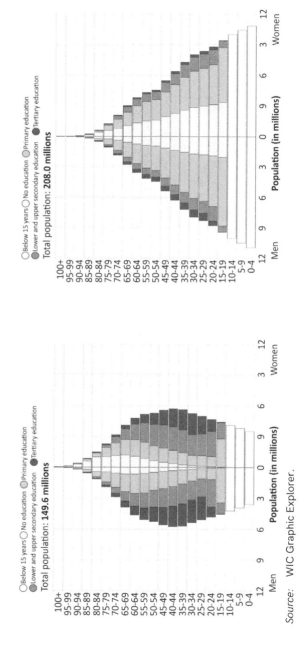

Source: WIC Graphic Explorer.

Figure 4.3   Age and educational pyramid for Ethiopia in 2060, SSP1 (left), SSP3 (right)

or a university. Within about half a century younger Ethiopians would then be roughly as well educated as Europeans are now. The population would continue to grow in this scenario; this is because of the currently very young population, and the fact that the demographic transition will take some time. But there would be "only" 150 million Ethiopians in 2060. By this time the number of children per woman would have fallen to its current level in Europe, so that an end of population growth in Ethiopia could be achieved by 2070. In the other extreme of scenario SSP3, the successes of the previous expansion of education would not be lost for the cohorts that already went to school. But for the ever-increasing successor cohorts, there would be no improvement. This would mean an increase in the absolute number of young people without any education. Under these conditions the fertility rate would only slow to about three children per woman by 2060 and increase the population to 278 million. Later in the century the difference in population size between the contrasting scenarios would increase to a factor of more than two.

What the future will look like is of course uncertain. The scenarios only can describe alternative developments that are not impossible in the sense that they are internally consistent and the path there is not entirely implausible. What is certain is that the lives of Ethiopians would be much worse under SSP3 conditions. Beyond social and economic stagnation, poor development outcomes may increasingly frustrate the growing population and exacerbate ethnic tensions and political crises as well as problems in adapting to already unavoidable climate change.

Human capital strengthens resilience to climate change

Future demographic trends, including human capital, matter greatly for different aspects of sustainable development. They are a key determinant of future resilience and adaptive capacity to potentially disruptive changes, including global climate change. Due to the insight that some degree of climate change is already ongoing and somewhat more unavoidable for the future, the attention of research has shifted from an earlier almost exclusive focus on mitigation to studying adaptation and differential vulnerability to climate change. But the approach taken is often misleading when, for certain parts of the world, the forecasted future climate conditions are matched with present-day socio-economic conditions (IPCC, 2014). We know for sure that not only the climate is changing but that societies are also changing over time and that aspects of social development such as public health capabilities are essential for their adaptive capacity. Disregarding such future social change would be misleading. It has been demonstrated recently that education is a key determinant of differential vulnerability both at the individual and societal level (Butz et al., 2014). Hence, the set of SSP scenarios offers an effective way for forecasting societies' future adaptive capacities to climate change (Lutz & Muttarak, 2017). Contrasting the SSP1 and SSP3 scenarios for the rest of the century (Lutz, Muttarak, et al., 2014) it has been shown that due to the educational expansion under the rapid social development path in SSP1, disaster mortality will be much lower – even in the case of increasing climate-related hazards – than in the SSP3 scenario where slower progress in education leads to high population growth and heightened vulnerability. Given the uncertainty about the precise manifestations of climate change in specific areas, there is a strong case to be made for general empowerment through education, which increases human and social capital to flexibly and effectively react to upcoming challenges rather than investing in massive concrete infrastructure projects that may turn out to be unproductive or otherwise problematic investments.

More generally, for the interactions of humans with environmental change, education has been shown to matter for behavioral changes necessary to mitigate human impacts such as changing behaviors in terms of choosing greener technologies, switching to public transport or recycling waste (Lutz & Muttarak, 2017). Since education improves knowledge, understanding of complex information, efficiency in allocation of resources and capacity to plan for the future (Cutler & Lleras-Muney, 2010; Kenkel, 1991; van der Pol, 2011) it is conducive for making better choices at the individual and societal level that will make a transition toward sustainability more likely.

The fact that the global environmental change research community has eagerly picked up these multi-dimensional demographic scenarios as being more relevant for understanding the challenges for sustainable development than in the previous focus on total population size alone, underlines the major claim of this book that multi-dimensional demography helps to make demography a discipline more relevant for the rest of the world.

Aging, dependency ratios and migration

In the late phases of the universal process of demographic transition when fertility rates are at low levels – often well below the so-called replacement level fertility of two surviving children per woman – and life expectancies are at high levels and continue to increase, significant changes in the age structure with a relative increase of elderly and a relative decline of younger age groups are a natural consequence. This change in the age structure is thus the combined consequence of the highly welcome decline in premature mortality and the associated increase in the average life span of people and the equally welcome fact that fertility is essentially within the realm of conscious choice and the proportion of unintended pregnancies has significantly declined. Whether the resulting fertility level is considered as too low, still too high, just right or simply accepted as the aggregate outcome of the sum of free reproductive decisions made by women and couples is a matter of judgement and the criteria used to assess what are the consequences of the given fertility levels. Having a closer look at these criteria is the focus of this section.

In a nutshell, there can be no doubt that Europe's population is, on average, getting older, at least if age is defined in the conventional way as time since birth, which does not factor in the trend of increasing life expectancy and better health and increasing education. In many respects, today "70 is the new 60". New demographic indicators have been developed to address this changing meaning of age. One such new indicator is the proportion of persons that have a remaining life expectancy of 15 or fewer years, an indicator that increases much more slowly than the proportion above age 65 in times of increasing life expectancy (Sanderson & Scherbov, 2005, 2010). Despite this, the proportion of the population that is above the chronological age of 65 is still widely considered a critical indicator. At the level of the EU-28 (still including the UK) this proportion is projected to increase from 18.2 percent currently to around 30 percent by 2050, which has given rise to widespread fears about negative economic and fiscal consequences of this demographic trend. As a consequence, either increased immigration or efforts in family policies to help increase fertility have been suggested – by different sides of the political spectrum – as possible policies to counteract population aging. But here we will show, under a multi-dimensional demographic approach, that neither of these two strategies pursued within realistic bounds will have as much impact as possible changes in labor force participation, improving educational attainment and better education and economic integration of immigrants.

Individual aging versus change in population age structure

The above described change in the population's age structure is also frequently labeled as "population aging" and measured either in terms of changes in the mean or median age of the population or the proportions above certain ages such as 60 or 65. Although this notion is common usage today and I have used it frequently in my own writings as shorthand for the longer reference to increasing proportions of people in higher age groups, I have recently become more critical about this notion because, in itself, neutral process of changing age structure has been given a clearly negative connotation. Aging is first and foremost a process that happens over the lifetime of individuals, with age measured as time since birth. While, over the first years of life, getting older is associated with gaining more strength, maturity and wisdom, in the later phases of the life course people tend to get gradually weaker until they eventually die. While in a strict sense we are also aging in the first parts of our lives, the notion of aging is generally associated with weakening and the increasing prevalence of sickness in the later parts of life. Since such ailing and getting nearer to death is an unwelcome part of aging, the notion gained a clearly negative connotation. But is it appropriate and legitimate to transfer this notion of aging from individuals to populations? Unlike individuals, populations do not have a lifecycle from birth to maturing to aging to death. Through population renewal, births ensure that populations become, in principle, immortal and it also makes no sense to speak of immature populations or old populations in an analogy to the individual lifecycle.

Why has the term "population aging" then become so popular? While this is hard to prove, there are reasons to assume that this analogy from the individual weakening through aging to the weakening of entire populations through lower proportions of young people was intentionally introduced by people deeply concerned about the implications of low fertility, in particular in France. Alfred Sauvy, the highly influential French demographer and founder of the French National Institute for Demographic Studies (INED) did not invent the term (in his 1966 book he cites a 1948 book by J. Daric on "Vieillissemant de la population") but eagerly picks up the notion to highlight the benefits of higher fertility. After discussing many of the problems associated with a demographic aging Sauvy writes: "Western societies must become conscious of this trend, which will only be evil if it is ignored. ... There is an obvious antidote: not to let fertility weaken..." (Sauvy, 1969, p. 319). Over time, the term "population aging" has gradually been picked up (uncritically) by demographers and in consequence by the general public. While most demographers tend to apply it in a more technical way using the above-described indicators, it has certainly maintained its negative connotation of aging associated with a weakening. Whenever population aging is discussed it tends to come together with mention of "problems" or at least "challenges". And this negative view seems to have spread widely among commentators of all levels. Nearly always when *The Economist* writes about the rise of China it also mentions the "looming aging crisis" that might stop that rise. Occasionally, even the much less educated and less developed India, with a younger population owing to higher fertility, is for this reason seen as having a much brighter future than rapidly aging China. These are conjectures without any solid scientific reasoning, presumably mostly based on the negative connotation associated with the notion of population aging and the overly simplistic associated notion of age dependency. In this sense, Sauvy has fully achieved what he may have intended.

When talking about scientific reasoning in terms of the consequences of an older age structure, a very simple demographic ratio – the so-called old-age dependency ratio calculated as the population aged 65+ divided by the population aged 15–64 – is usually taken as the proof for such claims. Because the use of dependency ratios lies at the very heart of the aging concerns, in this section we will directly focus on it and show that the conventional exclusively age-based ratios are insufficient and even misleading when trying to study the economic implications of population aging. We will again show that applying a multi-dimensional demographic approach which explicitly incorporates labor force participation and education as a proxy for productivity shows a very different and much more optimistic picture of the future than only looking at the age structure. We will study this in combination with addressing another highly controversial demographic topic, namely the issue of migration. We will show how the use of multi-dimensional demographic micro-simulation tools – modeling large numbers of individuals with different characteristics and their transition rates depending on these characteristics – can help us assess the longer-term effects of different future immigration patterns to the European Union and their consequences on different types of dependency ratios. The analysis is based on a study by Marois et al. (2020) published in 2020 in the pages of the *Proceedings of the National Academy of Sciences* (PNAS).[3]

Ever since the publication of an influential 2001 study by the United Nations on "replacement migration" (United Nations, 2001) this notion has prominently entered the public as well as the scientific debate over migration. This terminology has evidently been inspired by the notion of replacement-level fertility, a rather technical term in demography, referring to the level of fertility which, after adjusting for child mortality, would result in two children surviving to reproductive age per woman and thus, in the absence of migration and future changes in mortality, would result in a stationary population size and structure in the long run. Replacement migration in this sense refers to the international migration that a country would need in order to offset population decline and aging resulting from fertility rates that are lower than replacement-level. Although the United Nations study itself dealt with this in a purely numerical and rather neutral way, the implicit underlying assumption motivating the study was that population decline and increases in the so-called old-age dependency ratio (persons aged 65+/15–64) have negative consequences that should be avoided. The study illustrated under which hypothetical future migration patterns these consequences could be avoided.

In this new study (Marois et al., 2020) we also try to stay neutral with respect to specific policy recommendations. Instead we only try to demonstrate the implications of alternative migration and labor force participation scenarios on different dependency ratios, but we base our study on a much richer multi-dimensional model. While the 2001 study only considered age as a relevant human characteristic, in our micro-simulation model we use 13 characteristics of individuals (including among others labor force participation, duration of stay in the country, region of birth, education and level of mother's education). Another innovation of this paper is that it assesses demographic outcomes of the alternative scenarios in terms of three different dependency ratios that not only cover the changing age structure, but also changing patterns of labor force participation and productivity as approximated by level of education. Based on the still widely used conventional old-age dependency ratio – which considers everybody aged 15–64 as equally productive and all people above age 65 as unproductive – the presumed aging burden associated with an increase in this ratio is widely seen as a major economic problem leading to higher social security costs, relatively lower economic growth or even stagnation and decline. But such a simplistic approach based on age structure alone is outdated and partly misleading (Keyfitz, 1979; Lutz, Amran, Bélanger, et al., 2019; Lutz & KC, 2011; F. Willekens, 1978).

Different dependency ratios

We address the issue of dependency at three different levels of increasing complexity.

1. The *conventional age dependency ratio* (ADR) is defined as the ratio between the children and the elderly (0–14 + 65 and older) in the numerator and the so-called working-age population (15–64) in the denominator. This indicator only reflects the age structure of the population. This ratio is only a very crude approximation of actual economic dependency because not everybody starts to work at age 15, not everybody between ages 15 and 64 is working and not everybody age 65 and over is unproductive. For this reason, another ratio directly relates the people not in the labor force to those in the labor force:

2. The *labor force dependency ratio* (LFDR) has all economically inactive persons in the numerator and the active ones in the denominator. One should note that under the labor force concept as usually defined, all people currently in work (full or part time) or looking for work are considered as economically active. In other words, the labor force is the sum of men and women of all ages that are either employed or unemployed and looking for a job. It comes much closer to the real economic dependency than the ADR, for which reason it is sometimes called the "economic dependency ratio", which also occasionally includes the unemployed in the denominator as a "burden" on the employed. But since unemployment rates tend to be much more volatile (with seasonal variations and other short-term fluctuations) and precise definitions of unemployment vary from country to country, the LFDR is mostly preferred for longer-term international comparisons. While the LFDR clearly captures the true economic dependency more accurately than the ADR, the assumption that every member of the labor force equally contributes is still rather crude. Indeed, many argue that the fiscal impact of a decline of the labor force size could be compensated by an increase in overall productivity, which is highly correlated with education (Börsch-Supan Axel, 2003; Lee &

Mason, 2010; Ludwig et al., 2012; Prskawetz & Hammer, 2019). To take account of the fact that not all members of the labor force equally contribute to the economy, in this study we propose an innovative dependency indicator:

3. *The productivity-weighted labor force dependency ratio* (PWLFDR) builds on the LFDR and, in addition, approximates differences in productivity through wage differentials associated with various levels of educational attainment. As is usually done in economic studies, empirically assessed wage differentials are assumed to capture differentials in productivity which, in our case, have been estimated from the European Labor Force Surveys. The resulting education-specific productivity differentials are then maintained over time and superimposed to the multi-dimensional population scenarios by age, sex, education and labor force participation. Since these are four demographic dimensions as discussed above, their changing distributions over time and across populations will provide an even more accurate picture of changing dependency over time as resulting from demographic change.

Figure 4.4 shows that the three different indicators of dependency have very different projected trajectories in the EU under the same scenario (Baseline) that assumes middle-of-the-road fertility, mortality, migration, education and labor force participation up to 2060. In order to facilitate a better comparison of the trends over time, the three indicators have been standardized to 1.0 in 2015. Over the coming decades the conventional age dependency ratio shows the most dramatic increase of more than 60 percent by 2060. The increase even accelerates somewhat after 2025 due to the large baby boom generation reaching age 65. When focusing on the labor force dependency ratio, the increase gets much weaker (only 20 percent), partly as a consequence of the already embedded increase among younger cohorts in participation rates of women in the baseline scenario, and the increasing share of the more educated who also maintain higher participation rates, thus increasing the overall labor force participation. Finally, once we also consider the increases in productivity through the improving educational composition of the population, the result shows further reductions in the projected burden. Thus, despite the widespread fear of huge increases in dependency resulting from an increasing proportion of elderly, as generally transmitted by studies based solely on the future evolution of the age structure, for the productivity-weighted dependency ratio even under the baseline scenario

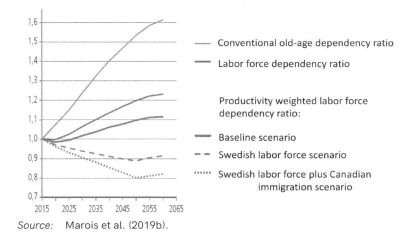

Source: Marois et al. (2019b).

Figure 4.4   Projected trends of different demographic dependency ratios in the EU based on age structure alone, considering labor-force participation and also adjusting for differential productivity by level of education. The broken line shows the case of all EU states converging to the labor-force pattern already observed in Sweden, and the dotted line also assumes immigration patterns as currently observed in Canada

(continuation of status quo) our results show a quite modest 10 percent increase by 2060.

Migration and labor force participation scenarios

The study defined a set of six alternative scenarios that also reflect different possible policy directions for all 28 member states of the European Union (still including the UK as of 2019) with respect to volume of immigration, selectivity of migrants in terms of education and efforts made to integrate migrants into the labor force. These scenarios, with different migration-related assumptions, are assessed against the background of possible future trends in labor force participation of the general population by either assuming a continuation of the recent trend or assuming that all EU member states move towards the pattern of much higher participation, which is already observed in Sweden today. Figure 4.5 illustrates this Swedish pattern and contrasts it against the current pattern in Italy, where at all ages people – in particular women – participate less in the labor force. Also, in comparison, the age at retirement is much higher in Sweden.

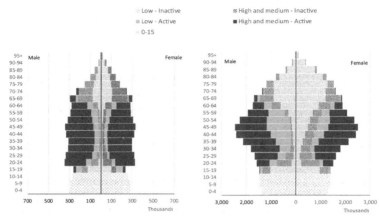

Source: Marois et al. (2019b).

Figure 4.5   Age pyramids by labor-force participation and education for Sweden (left) and Italy (right) for 2015

Using a multi-dimensional population projection model by a micro-simulation called CEPAM-Mic (Bélanger et al., 2019; Marois et al., 2019a, 2019b; Potančoková & Marois, 2020), which also considers the duration of stay in the destination country and the age at immigration, we built different scenarios of changes in labor force participation rates, the number of immigrants, their composition and their integration into the labor market in an effort to measure the impact of different policies on projected dependency ratios for 2015–2060.

The study specifies a set of six different scenarios with respect to future migration and labor force participation trends. Here we will only highlight three of these.

i. The *Baseline scenario* assuming "business as usual", i.e. a continuation of past trends in terms (about 10 million immigrants over 5 years combined with constant out-migration rates, resulting in a net migration gain of roughly 4.6 million over 5 years) of constant migrant compositions and integration, and a continuation of recent trends in labor force participation for native-born.

ii. The *Swedish Labor Force scenario* assumes gradual increases up to 2050 in labor force participation rates, in particular among women and elderly, to the levels already observed in Sweden today. Sweden is the country where participation rates are among the highest in Europe. Thus, this scenario shows the effect of efficient policies seeking to increase the labor force participation. All other assumptions are equal to the Baseline Scenario.

iii. The *Swedish Labor Force plus Canadian Immigration scenario* tests the additional effect of a more selective immigration system as in Canada (for the EU, 20 million over 5 years, which corresponds to the Canadian immigration rate in the last quarter of a century).

The results confirm the view that when assessing the relative impact of various migration and integration scenarios in terms of the resulting changes in economic dependency, the underlying changes in labor force participation of the total population hold a large influence (Bijak et al., 2008; Rees et al., 2012). Figure 4.4 shows the projected trends in the productivity-weighted labor force dependency ratio for the EU up to 2060 under the three different scenarios described above. A convergence of labor force participation rates to what is currently observed in Sweden would be enough to completely reverse the trend and to expect a decrease in the dependency ratio by 10 percent (broken line in Figure 4.4). Combined with high Canadian immigration levels that is selective for high education, the productivity-weighted dependency ratio in the EU would even decline by 20 percent over the coming decades, despite of the strong increase of the population above the age of 65 (dotted line in Figure 4.4).

It is also instructive to briefly summarize the results of other scenarios that have not been included in the presentation here: a Canadian scenario, which assumes high immigration rates of better educated migrants combined with a better integration of them into the labor market than is the case currently in Canada, produces results very close to the Swedish Labor Force scenario, even if it maintains the country-specific labor force participation rates. The Canadian scenario, assuming high immigration of well-educated people combined with intermediate integration into the labor force (close to the current situation in Canada), results essentially in a flat line of no future change in economic dependency. Conversely, a combination of high immigration volumes with low education and unsuccessful integration results in a sizeable increase in the dependency burden of 20 percent, twice the increase of the baseline scenario. This clearly illustrates that high immigration by itself will not have positive impacts on future dependency, with the impact greatly depending on education and speed of integration into the labor force.

This analysis shows that the policy conclusion drawn with respect to a possible "demographic need" for migrants in Europe changes markedly when different sources of population heterogeneity and associated dependency burdens are considered in a multi-dimensional context. The conventional way of only considering the changing age composition of the population has served as the foundation for the above-mentioned United Nations study on "Replacement Migration" (United Nations, 2001), which concluded that migration can help avoid population decline but that a stop in the increase of the total age dependency ratio would require implausibly high volumes of immigrants and would therefore be unrealistic. In our study, a very different picture has appeared when adding labor force participation and education as additional demographic characteristics to the analysis. It shows that the projected dependency ratios will increase much less than previously expected under baseline trend assumptions. When the model also covers the effect of education on productivity and not only on labor force participation the projected increase in burden under the baseline scenario is only a low 10 percent by 2060. This implies that indeed much of the fears associated with an increasing proportion of elderly seem exaggerated. As this increase is modest, either moderate migration levels, if migrants are well-educated and integrated, or an increase in labor force participation among the general population can more than compensate for it.

Under the Canadian migration scenario – high volume of well-educated immigrants, but with intermediate integration – the European Union would experience virtually no increase in this dependency ratio accounting for labor force participation and productivity. If large numbers of low educated migrants enter and the labor force integration of migrants deteriorates, however, the EU's dependency ratio would worsen by a significant 20 percent increase. This shows the high stakes involved with integration outcomes under high migration volumes.

Although an increase in the proportion of the population above age 65 is unavoidable in Europe, the analysis presented here shows that the fears associated with the coming economic burden have been unduly exaggerated through the use of the simplistic and inappropriate conventional age dependency ratio. There are plausible scenarios under which feasible public policies could be effective in coping with the consequences of these changes in age structure. Europe actually has a portfolio of policy options to choose from, ranging from encouraging higher labor force participation among the native population to education selective migration together with high integration efforts. With the right social policies Europe can likely avoid the widely assumed negative impacts of a higher proportion of people above the current retirement ages and maintain a dynamic labor force based on high human capital.

As a consequence of these insights, I would suggest changing the terminology used and trying to avoid the notion of population aging with its clearly negative connotation, which is unsubstantiated, and opt for more neutral terms, such as changing age structure or changing demographic structures, the latter in our definition also includes the highly desirable increases in educational attainment, labor force participation and thus human capital. This also suggests that public policies trying to influence demographic trends with the goal of improving the longer-term well-being of the population should not only target the conventional mortality/health, fertility and migration factors but be framed in the broader multi-dimensional context of strengthening human capital by managing the human resource base for sustainable development, as will be discussed in the following section.

Population policies: human resource management for sustainable development

The discipline of demography has always been linked to policy concerns. From its very beginning with John Graunt's "Bills of Mortality" in 1661, where the concern was the improvement of public health, to Robert Malthus' 1798 "Essay on the Principle of Population", where the concern was essentially how to limit population growth to avoid mass starvation, demographic techniques and models were developed primarily to assist public policies to have a stronger scientific basis for making policy choices. This focus of demography as a discipline is very much in line with defining demography as an intervention science, as was discussed in Chapter 2.

The rise of modern demography in the 20th century was also closely associated with fears of the consequences of population decline in some European countries, as well as fears of population growth at the global level. It is indicative that the first international scientific conference on population assembled in Geneva in 1927, which subsequently led to the foundation of the International Union for the Scientific Study of Population (IUSSP), had the following text in its announcement:

> The World Population Conference represents a pioneer effort on an international scale to grapple with one of the most fundamental problems which mankind faces today. The earth, and every geographical division of it, is strictly limited in size and in ability to support human populations. But these populations keep on growing; and in so doing they are creating social, economic and political situations which threaten to alter profoundly our present civilization, and perhaps ultimately to wreck it. (Margret Sanger, *Proceedings of the World Population Conference 1927*, London 1927, p. 5; cited in Caldwell & Caldwell, 1986, pp. 8–9)

The most significant period of growth of demography as an independent scientific discipline occurred in the 1950s and 1960s, mostly in the USA and with targeted funding from American foundations such as the Ford and Rockefeller Foundations to establish population studies centers at many leading American universities (Caldwell & Caldwell, 1986). Again, the motivation for these major investments in demography was mostly related to population policies with the goal of turning the attention of American social scientists to population-growth-related issues in developing countries and to train many young experts from those countries. At the same time, several population research and training centers were established throughout Asia, Latin America and Africa. The clear objective of these efforts was to reduce rapid population growth through family planning programs. As the 20th century entered its last decade, the political climate for population policies started to change. The International Conference on Population and Development (ICPD) in Cairo in 1994 called for a shift from the previous population control approaches to concerns about the rights of women and their reproductive health, or more generally viewed the health and welfare of individuals as the only legitimate goal of population policies (May, 2012). The need to empower women through education and economic opportunities was expressed as a goal of population policies. But as stressed by Sinding (2005), IPCD 1994 has probably unintentionally contributed to delegitimizing state interventions and active-government led population policies of any kind. Ever since Cairo, the right to operate through public interventions in what was deemed to be the realm of private citizens' lives has been challenged, or, in other words, proponents of individual reproductive rights and freedom have gained the upper hand and discussions of macro-demographic issues have been largely delegitimized (May, 2012).

While the above-described discussion has largely concerned possible interventions in high fertility countries to speed up the fertility transition, there has been an opposite current of concern building up in some countries that have already experienced significant increases in the proportion of their elderly population and in some cases population decline. In particular, in some Eastern European countries the combination of low fertility, still rather high mortality and significant out-migration, has given rise to serious concerns of depopulation. According to the president of Serbia, depopulation is the country's single most important problem for the future (source: personal conversation with President Vucic). For these kinds of concerns the Cairo Program of Action has little to offer. These are macro-level concerns that cannot simply be addressed in terms of individual rights. Macro-level challenges also require policy responses with intended macro-level consequences while at the same time respecting individual level rights.

What looks like a contradiction in goals without an obvious solution – i.e., individual freedom versus state intervention to influence population size – can be quite easily resolved once we move to the level of multi-dimensional demography and also introduce education, health status and labor force participation into the policy model. In a paper entitled "A population policy rationale for the 21st century" (Lutz, 2014a), I introduced a focus on human capital and national human resource management – in analogy to the human resource management of companies – as a population policy rationale that can simultaneously address the concerns around high population growth as well as about aging and depopulation while at the same time assuring individual rights and freedom. But before we discuss this proposed new goal of population policies in more detail, we have to address the conventional macro-level goal that still seems to be ubiquitous in the minds of most demographers, policymakers and journalists, namely that 2.1 children per woman would somehow be the most desirable fertility level.

Replacement level fertility is not a meaningful goal to aim at

The notion that replacement level fertility (on average two surviving children per woman) would somehow be optimal seems to be ubiquitous. When asked about what a desirable fertility level for populations might be, most politicians, journalists and even demographers would spontaneously answer that it is slightly above two children per woman, or often even the precise number of a Total Fertility Rate (TFR) of 2.1. As justification for this specific level of fertility people usually refer to some vague notion of stabilizing population size, or the age dependency ratio, or maintaining the size of the working age population. But a closer look at the demographic models that underlie this reasoning reveals that this supposedly precise level of 2.1 (actually more like 2.06 under low mortality conditions) is only derived from a highly stylized theoretical model of stationary population. It has little to do with actually maintaining the size of the labor force in contemporary *real* societies. All of these populations tend to have quite irregular age structures and the size of the working age population is influenced by migration and mortality changes in addition to fertility. However, even in the hypothetical absence of migration and under constant mortality conditions, in countries with a high share of young people (positive momentum of population growth), fertility needs to be well below replacement level if the goal is to keep the absolute size of the working age population constant. Conversely, in countries with relatively few younger people (i.e. that have already entered a phase of negative momentum), fertility needs to be significantly above replacement level, if again the goal is to maintain the working age population. Lutz et al. (2003) showed that Europe's population entered the phase of negative momentum around the year 2000. Hence, in this context of real European populations and their empirically given age structures, a reference to replacement level fertility makes little sense even in terms of the stated goal of maintaining the population aged 15–64 in its current size. On top of this, all real populations in Europe and elsewhere do experience mortality change and migration and hence render the 2.1 goal even less relevant as a way to achieve the supposedly desirable stationary demographic situation. And, as discussed in the previous section, the so-called working age population is only a poor proxy for the actual labor force and its productivity.

Recently, there have been two independent strains of research that both come to the conclusion that, for most countries in the world, long-term fertility levels somewhat below replacement level would be preferable to replacement level fertility for economic reasons. One is based on an extension of the National Transfer Accounts (NTA) approach which collected empirical data for over 40 countries for age-specific consumption and income profiles (Lee & Mason, 2011). In a recent study this NTA approach is combined with an economic model showing that population decline actually increases the capital/output ratio, and hence a moderate shrinking of the population leads to higher consumption and also welfare. While, from a pure fiscal/public finance point of view, the model shows that fertility should be significantly above replacement, combining this with the goal of maximizing consumption yields a much lower desirable long-term TFR: 1.24 for today's low income countries, 1.50 for the middle income group, and 1.79 for the high income group (Lee & Mason, 2012).

A different line of research focusing on the heterogeneity of the population with respect to education, and the fact that better educated persons cost more due to education investments during the early phases of life but are then more productive later in life, arrives at very similar conclusions. Striessnig and Lutz (2013) systematically assess this issue of "optimal fertility" by first defining and discussing a number of optimality criteria and then presenting extensive sets of simulations about the implications of alternative long-term fertility levels on education-weighted support ratios, which also factor in the costs and benefits of education. Under this model, the long-term optimal fertility level (assumed to minimize the dependency burden) turns out to be well below replacement level fertility, with the optimum around TFRs 1.5–1.8. This is for a population assumed to be closed to migration and with life expectancy gradually increasing. If migration gains were to be included in the model, the optimal fertility level would fall even lower.

In a subsequent article (Striessnig & Lutz, 2014), the authors go one step further and include additional externalities to childbearing, such as emissions contributing to global climate change. When their model is combined with the PET (Population-Environment-Technology) model by O'Neill et al. (2010), which translates alternative population trajectories resulting from different fertility levels into trajectories of carbon emissions, the optimal fertility comes out much lower and greatly depends on what weight is given to the goal of minimizing emissions versus minimizing the aging burden. The higher the weight given to climate change the lower the optimal level of fertility turns out to be.

Viewed together, these calculations suggest that current fertility levels in most European countries (after adjusting for their downward tempo distortions) are not too far from their optimum, provided that societies continue to invest in education, and this also results in higher productivity. At the country level, the calculations lead to politically sensitive conclusions: following this rationale the current German fertility level is about right but that of France is too high to be optimal. These results are obtained even without considering the impacts of immigration and with giving only minimal weight to carbon emissions. If climate change is given a higher weight, then most countries of Europe and, in particular, the United States, can be viewed as having too high fertility even under optimistic assumptions about future transitions to green technologies.

Whether or not the model assumptions made by Striessnig and Lutz are being accepted, this analysis, together with the above mentioned studies by Lee and Mason (2012) and Bongaarts and Sobotka (2012), who showed that in Europe migration gains compensate in part for the age structural effects of low fertility, make it clear that the ubiquitous view that replacement level fertility should be considered as ideal is far from self-evident and needs to be reconsidered.

Sometimes the argument is put forward that, in the very long run, i.e. many centuries into the future, any constant fertility level other than replacement level – assuming that mortality does not further change – would result in either an explosion or the disappearance of the human race. But, first of all, fertility rates are very unlikely to remain constant over long periods and with respect to population-related policies several centuries are too long as a planning horizon. As discussed before, Gietel-Basten et al. (2013) have shown that a global level of a TFR of 1.75 from 2050 onwards would, by 2300, result in a world population size of 3–4 billion people depending on the assumed future trend in life expectancy. If global fertility were to converge to a TFR of 1.5 then by 2200 the world population would be around 3 billion. This is similar to the world population size in the 1960s. And many ecologists seem to consider a total population size of 3 billion as desirable from an environmental perspective (Barrett et al., 2020). And what would bring the world to a population of 3 billion would be strong investments in female education which – as discussed above – would also help to increase resilience to already unavoidable environmental change. With reference to the above-mentioned very long-term population scenarios, I recently summarized the global outlook as follows: towards a world of 2–4 billion well-educated and therefore healthy and wealthy people who would be able to cope well with the consequences of already unavoidable climate change (Lutz, 2017b).

Strengthening women's rights and health through education

In the previous chapters we have discussed overwhelming evidence that education of girls plays a key role in improving health, bringing down high fertility rates, strengthening gender equity within families and in society and even enhancing economic growth and strengthening resilience. These are all important reasons for putting education right at the heart of a 21st century population policy approach.

With respect to international policy processes in the context of the United Nations, the multi-dimensional demographic approach taken here has important implications for interpreting the ICPD Programme of Action agreed in Cairo in 1994, which has been widely seen as doing away with quantitative demographic targets altogether and replacing them by a focus on individual human rights, gender equity and reproductive health. However, advances in the average educational attainment of women as well as in aggregate level measures of health and female status are fully in line with ICPD and, under our definition, also qualify as demographic targets. In other words, there can be aggregate level quantitative demographic targets under this approach, even if they do not directly focus on reaching certain fertility levels or population growth rates. A priority focus on human capital formation with a special emphasis on girls' education will bring most of the desired macro-level outcomes. In this spirit, the UK government has recently announced that it decided to make girls' education its priority foreign policy objective over the coming years (BFPG, 2020).

It is important to understand that population policies must not be seen in isolation. IPCD and its reaffirmation in the Cairo+20 and Cairo+25 meetings are embedded in the larger framework of international development goals. In 2000, the global community assembled by the United Nations agreed on a set of eight development goals, the so-called Millennium Development Goals (MDGs). They gave specific quantitative goals for ending extreme poverty and hunger, reducing child mortality, improving gender equity, and achieving universal primary education for all boys and girls around the world by 2015. These goals were mostly developed top-down by experts in international agencies and largely focused on progress in developing countries without paying much attention to climate change and other environmental changes that were addressed in different international frameworks. This was very different from the process leading up to the 2015 Sustainable Development Goals (SDGs), which were developed during one of the broadest structured discussion processes so far with a great involvement of civil society around the world. They also combined social, economic, and environmental goals and were addressing all countries of the world, including rich industrialized countries.

The United Nations set up an Independent Group of Scientists (IGS) to monitor, assess progress and point at possible new challenges in the implementation of the SDGs. The first of the quadrennial Global Sustainable Development Reports come out in 2019 under the title, "The Future is Now: Science for Achieving Sustainable Development" (Independent Group of Scientists appointed by the Secretary-General, 2019). As one of the 15 independent scientists invited by the United Nations Secretary General to produce this report, I was also involved in discussions as how to view population policies in the context of these much broader policy goals. While population growth is not explicitly mentioned in the SDGs, several of the SDGs are directly or indirectly related to future demographic trends. The SDGs related to child mortality, maternal mortality, causes of death and reproductive health as well as the very ambitious goals on universal primary and secondary education and gender equity can be translated into future mortality and fertility pathways. This report also specifies as its first entry point the strengthening of human well-being and capabilities.

In the following I will try to briefly summarize a quantification of the consequences on long-term global population growth of reaching the relevant education and health targets as given in the SDGs (Abel et al., 2016). While mortality and related goals directly affect future mortality trends, if achieved, improvements in educational attainment resulting from the education goal affect fertility and mortality trends in an indirect way. As discussed in the previous chapter, consistently, better educated women experience lower fertility and lower child mortality – in particular during the process of demographic transition – and better educated men and women exhibit higher life expectancies. SDG4's aims to "ensure inclusive and equitable quality education and promote life-long learning opportunities for all" consists of ten targets. The most specific of these targets (4.1) states that "by 2030, ensure that all girls and boys complete free, equitable and quality primary and secondary education leading to relevant and effective learning outcomes". This is also the target that can be directly translated into demographic outcomes in the context of the multi-dimensional population projections methodology. It is also important to note that universal primary education has already been part of the earlier MDGs and the addition of universal secondary education in the SDGs is new and much more ambitious. This is partly based on recent insights that for poor countries to come out of poverty, universal primary education is not enough; it must be complemented by secondary education of broad segments of the population (Lutz et al., 2008).

The SDG scenarios as defined in this study by Abel et al. (2016) result in a world population that still increases to 8.8 to 9.1 billion by mid-century and then levels off and starts a moderate decline to between 8.2 and 9.0 billion by 2100. This is significantly below the medium variant of the United Nations population projections, which reaches 9.7 billion in 2050 and 11.2 billion in 2100. In fact, the SDG scenario even lies below the lower bound of the 95 percent uncertainty interval of the United Nations probabilistic population projections, which raises some issues of consistency of messages within the United Nations system. This lower global population trajectory is primarily caused by the accelerated fertility declines associated with the female education and reproductive health goals in Africa and Western Asia. In terms of the SSP scenarios it comes to lie between the middle-of-the-road SSP2 scenario and the SSP1 rapid development scenario, which assumes unusually rapid progress until the end of the century, while the SDG scenario only assumes a "turbo" of development until 2030 followed by a return to a more middle-of-the-road speed of development.

While many demographers and people concerned about rapid population growth contributing to climate change have complained about population growth not being explicitly addressed in the SDGs (Barrett et al., 2020; Bongaarts & O'Neill, 2018), the above-described Abel et al. (2016) study shows that, indeed, the education and health targets included in the SDGs include just the right policy priorities in the sense that they will be, if implemented, effective in significantly curbing world population growth and, in addition, have many further benefits in terms of empowering women, contributing to poverty reduction and increasing general resilience. In addition, unlike a direct focus on fertility or population growth rates, a focus on female education and health is uncontroversial and fully in line with the Cairo agenda. A joint focus on female education and reproductive health services is likely to have a much stronger effect on fertility decline than an exclusive focus on meeting the unmet need for contraception in the case that women still have high desired family sizes because female education, particularly in countries in demographic transition, has a direct causal effect on lowering desired family size and, at the same time, empowering women within their families and in society to actually realize these lower fertility goals. Improving the availability of reproductive health services can then contribute to enhancing contraceptive prevalence for women who have already gone through the cognitive transition – as discussed in Chapter 2 – which leads them to move from largely uncontrolled fertility to conscious family limitation. Since universal primary and secondary education of all young women around the world is a prominent goal in its own right (SDG 4) and is politically unproblematic – except for a few fundamentalist groups that oppose girls' education – this focus on education provides a strong and convincing policy paradigm, which in addition to all the other beneficial consequences of education also leads to lower fertility.

Demographic resilience and national human resource management

The term resilience comes from the field of ecology where it was first introduced by Holling (1973), who defined it as a measure of the persistence of systems and their ability to absorb change and disturbance and still maintain the same relationships between populations or state variables. It is now widely used in the context of global environmental change. In the context of demography, it has recently been picked up by the regional office of the United Nations Population Fund (UNFPA) for Europe and Central Asia as a notion intended to provide a population policy framework in the context of the fact that many countries in the region are deeply concerned about depopulation and a rapidly changing age structure, a macro-level demographic concern for which the Cairo agenda focusing primarily on high fertility developing countries had little to offer.

This helplessness of the Cairo agenda and more conventional population policy approaches to deal with 21st century demographic challenges became apparent at the Cairo+20 review conference for the United Nations Economic Commission for Europe in Geneva, including 56 Northern countries from Vladivostok westward to Vancouver. All of these countries are well advanced in the process of demographic transition and thus experience rapid increases in the proportions of elderly, and, except for those with significant migration gains, many face the prospect of population shrinking. Bulgaria, for instance, has already experienced a population decline from around 9 million in 1990 to 7.2 million today, heading toward an estimated 6 million by 2030. Japan has also started to shrink and faces the prospect of losing 30 percent of its population over the coming decades, with the median age of the population increasing from 44 years now to above 55 in 2050. Efforts to turn around these trends through policies that directly enhance birth rates have been largely ineffective and are unlikely to change the big picture in the foreseeable future (Luci-Greulich & Thévenon, 2013; Stone, 2020). There is also concern around ethical questions as to whether it is acceptable to try to directly influence reproductive decisions or whether governments should respect these personal decisions and only focus on improving the conditions for raising children. This all called for a fundamentally new approach to population policy.

In the context of responding to this apparent need for population policies to address depopulation, the UNFPA has defined demographic resilience in the following way:

> Ensuring that societies can thrive in a world of rapid demographic change means moving beyond narrow quick-fix approaches focused on population numbers towards comprehensive population and social policies aimed at ensuring prosperity and well-being for all. They focus on social policies and programmes that respond to demographic change, strengthen human capital and shape a prosperous future. ... The programme thus helps foster demographically resilient societies that understand and anticipate the population dynamics they are experiencing, and ensure they have the skills, tools, political will and public support to manage them. In this way, countries can mitigate potentially negative effects for individuals, societies, economies and the envi-

ronment, and harness the opportunities that come with demographic change for people, prosperity and the planet. (UNFPA, 2020)

This focus on human resources as an integral part of population policies is slowly gaining momentum in the international discussions. The UNDP 2013 Human Development Report makes extensive reference to the need for integrated approaches incorporating education, health and population trends in international development strategies (UNDP, 2013). In 2012, a global interdisciplinary scientific panel on "Population and Sustainable Development" concluded the publication of its statement in *Science* with the sentence: "Invest in human capital – people's education and health, including reproductive health – to slow population growth, accelerate the transition to green technologies, and improve people's adaptive capacity to environmental change" (Lutz et al., 2012). While the focus of this panel was mostly on developing countries, its recommendations were designed to be of relevance for all countries of the world. And, finally, the SSP approached described in the previous section views the educational composition of the population as a key determinant of future mitigative and adaptive capacity to address climate change and its likely consequences for future human well-being.

Human capital and human resource management were also a prominent topic at the 2014 annual meeting of the World Economic Forum in Davos. Among other things, it was suggested that in analogy to private sector strategies, governments should develop a more integrated "Public Human Resource Management". This view was also captured in a piece I published in the *Harvard Business Review*, which says:

> Viewing the quality of human capital as resting on a collection of elements, many of them manageable, is something that the private sector has been doing for a long time. Every sizable business pays attention to human resource management. For governments the equivalent would be a form of national human resource management that considered education, migration, family, labor, health, and retirement as components that interact richly – and together drive the richness of the future. (Lutz, 2014b)

One decisive difference between public and private sector human resource management is, however, that states cannot fire people (at least not their own citizens). This is why states have social policies in addition to economic policies. But increasingly the goals of social policies also go in the direction of trying to empower people to help themselves, if at all possible. Or as the German education minister put it on the occasion of the 2012 annual assembly of the Max Planck Society: "Education policy is the social and economic policy of the 21st century" (Ministerium für Schule und Weiterbildung, 2012).

It has been argued (Lutz, 2017b) that the rise of human civilization over the millennia was driven by the proportion of the population that is able to read and write. And with literacy, the decisive changes in development came 500 years ago when, as part of the Reformation, Martin Luther demanded that all men and women, even of the lowest classes, should become literate in order to be able to read the Bible themselves. And this resulted in social and economic development, first, in the Protestant countries of Northern Europe and, subsequently, in the rest of Europe and of the world, as increasing proportions of the population – and, in particular, women – became literate. In this context, I also coined the notion of "*homo sapiens literata*" which I presented in the opening lecture to the 2018 general assembly of the Pontifical Academy of Sciences (Lutz, 2018), one of the most prestigious scientific academies with roots back to 1603. There, I tried to summarize recent findings in demographic and interdisciplinary research showing the central role of education of not just elites but the general public, including all women. This was a rather courageous step not only in terms of proclaiming a new human sub-species – which is legitimate in the context of cultural evolution as long as it marks a significant qualitative change that is essentially irreversible – but also because of the intentional use of the female gender of the adjective "literata" to homo, which in conventional Latin grammar has a male gender, although it refers to both men and women. The female gender was chosen to underline the decisive role of female literacy and education in the transformation of human societies.

Empowered *homo sapiens literata* has shaped the world, including not only an improvement in living conditions but also a visible footprint on the natural environment. This in turn also threatens to undermine our own life support systems in the future. But a focus on education and the knowledge and abstraction skills that come with it may offer opportunities for insight and foresight which can help bring about the necessary transformation towards sustainable development and, at the same time, strengthen our adaptive capacity to already unavoidable environmental changes. This has also been stressed in a statement of the German National Academy of Sciences Leopoldina on "Brainpower for sustainable development" in the context of the above mentioned Global Sustainable Development Report 2019 (Leopoldina, 2019).

While such considerations partly go beyond demography, many of the scientific insights they are based on result from the broader multi-dimensional approach to demography that is the focus of this "Advanced Introduction". The analysis of the implications of the changing composition of all populations around the world by age, gender, education and other relevant characteristics leads to the conclusion that the strengthening of human capital, beginning with and concentrating on education and health, should be the new global population and development policy paradigm, based on sound scientific evidence and the respect for individual human rights that is equally valid for all societies around the world. Such a new policy paradigm will certainly not be accepted overnight, but, as outlined above, it is slowly gaining momentum for a deeper and broader understanding of population policies in the context of sustainable development.

Notes

1. I remember well, being at the United Nations in New York on that day and addressing the delegations of United Nations member states at a special event organized by UNFPA about the implications of population growth for global sustainable development. It was also made very clear to the participants that the choice of picking this particular date was more symbolic rather than based on any direct measurement.
2. Here we essentially treat the notions of forecast and projections as synonymous, with forecast having a somewhat broader connotation as making statements about the future where its projection is more technical as related to specific projection models.
3. The rest of this section partly draws on this paper or newsletters that summarize its findings.

References

Abel, G. J., Barakat, B., KC, S., & Lutz, W. (2016). Meeting the Sustainable Development Goals leads to lower world population growth. *Proceedings of the National Academy of Sciences, 113*(50), 14294–14299. https://doi.org/10.1073/pnas.1611386113

Ahlburg, D. A., & Lutz, W. (1999). Introduction: The need to rethink approaches to population forecasts. In W. Lutz, J. W. Vaupel, & D. A. Ahlburg (Eds.), *Frontiers of Population Forecasting* (pp. 1–14). Population Council. https://www.jstor.org/stable/2808048

Aries, P. (1980). Two successive motivations for the declining birth rate in the west. *Population and Development Review, 6*(4), 645–650. https://doi.org/10.2307/1972930

Armstrong, J. S., & Collopy, F. (1992). Error measures for generalizing about forecasting methods: Empirical comparisons. *International Journal of Forecasting, 8*(1), 69–80. https://doi.org/10.1016/0169-2070(92)90008-W

Arthur, W. B., & Vaupel, J. W. (1983). *Some General Relationships in Population Dynamics* (IIASA Working Paper WP-83-89). IIASA. http://pure.iiasa.ac.at/id/eprint/2223/

Barrett, S., Dasgupta, A., Dasgupta, P., Adger, W. N., Anderies, J., Bergh, J. van den, Bledsoe, C., Bongaarts, J., Carpenter, S., Chapin, F. S., Crépin, A.-S., Daily, G., Ehrlich, P., Folke, C., Kautsky, N., Lambin, E. F., Levin, S. A., Mäler, K.-G., Naylor, R., ... Wilen, J. (2020). Social dimensions of fertility behavior and consumption patterns in the Anthropocene. *Proceedings of the National Academy of Sciences, 117*(12), 6300–6307. https://doi.org/10.1073/pnas.1909857117

Barro, R. J., & Sala-i-Martin, X. I. (2003). *Economic Growth* (2nd Edition). The MIT Press.

Basten, S., & Jiang, Q. (2015). Fertility in China: An uncertain future. *Population Studies, 69*(sup1), S97–S105. https://doi.org/10.1080/00324728.2014.982898

Becker, G. S. (1981). *A Treatise on the Family*. Harvard University Press.

Becker, G. S. (1993). *Human Capital: A Theoretical and Empirical Analysis, with Special Reference to Education*. University of Chicago Press. https://www.amazon.com/Human-Capital-Theoretical-Empirical-Reference/dp/0226041204

Becker, G. S., & Barro, R. J. (1988). A reformulation of the economic theory of fertility. *The Quarterly Journal of Economics, 103*(1), 1–25. https://doi.org/10.2307/1882640

Becker, G. S., Murphy, K. M., & Tamura, R. (1990). Human capital, fertility, and economic growth. *Journal of Political Economy, 98*(5, Part 2), S12–S37. https://doi.org/10.1086/261723

Bélanger, A., Sabourin, P., Marois, G., Van Hook, J., & Vézina, S. (2019). A framework for the prospective analysis of ethno-cultural super-diversity. *Demographic Research, 41*(11), 293–330.

Benhabib, J., & Spiegel, M. (1994). The role of human capital in economic development. Evidence from aggregate cross-country data. *Journal of Monetary Economics, 34*(2), 143–173. https://doi.org/10.1016/0304-3932(94)90047-7

Benhabib, J., & Spiegel, M. (2005). Human capital and technology diffusion. In *Handbook of Economic Growth* (Vol. 1, pp. 935–966). Elsevier.

BFPG. (2020). *Achieving the UK's Foreign Policy Objectives through Investment in Girls' Education*. British Foreign Policy Group. https://bfpg.co.uk/wp-content/uploads/2020/10/BFPG-Girls-Education-Report-October-2020-V2.pdf

Bhrolcháin, M. N., & Dyson, T. (2007). On causation in demography: Issues and illustrations. *Population and Development Review, 33*(1), 1–36. https://doi.org/10.1111/j.1728-4457.2007.00157.x

Bijak, J., Kupiszewska, D., & Kupiszewski, M. (2008). Replacement migration revisited: Simulations of the effects of selected population and labor market strategies for the aging Europe, 2002–2052. *Population Research and Policy Review, 27*(3), 321–342. https://doi.org/10.1007/s11113-007-9065-2

Blau, P. M., & Duncan, O. D. (1967). *The American Occupational Structure* (pp. xvii, 520). John Wiley & Sons.

Bloom, D. E., Canning, D., Fink, G., & Finlay, J. E. (2009). Fertility, female labor force participation, and the demographic dividend. *Journal of Economic Growth, 14*(2), 79–101. https://doi.org/10.1007/s10887-009-9039-9

Bloom, D. E., Sevilla, J., & Canning, D. (2003). *Demographic Dividend: New Perspective on Economic Consequences Population Change*. Rand Publishing.

Bloom, D. E., & Williamson, J. G. (1998). Demographic transitions and economic miracles in emerging Asia. *World Bank Economic Review, 12*(3), 419–455.

Bongaarts, J. (2008). What can fertility indicators tell us about pronatalist policy options? *Vienna Yearbook of Population Research, 6*, 39–55. https://doi.org/10.1553/populationyearbook2008s39

Bongaarts, J. (2010). The causes of educational differences in fertility in Sub-Saharan Africa. *Vienna Yearbook of Population Research, 8*, 31–50. JSTOR. https://doi.org/10.1553/populationyearbook2010s31

Bongaarts, J., & Hardee, K. (2019). Trends in contraceptive prevalence in Sub-Saharan Africa: The roles of family planning programs and education. *African Journal of Reproductive Health, 23*(3), Article 3. https://doi.org/10.29063/ajrh2019/v23i3.9

Bongaarts, J., & O'Neill, B. C. (2018). Global warming policy: Is population left out in the cold? *Science, 361*(6403), 650–652. https://doi.org/10.1126/science.aat8680

Bongaarts, J., & Sobotka, T. (2012). A demographic explanation for the recent rise in European fertility. *Population and Development Review, 38*(1), 83–120. https://doi.org/10.1111/j.1728-4457.2012.00473.x

Bongaarts, J., & Watkins, S. C. (1996). Social interactions and contemporary fertility transitions. *Population and Development Review, 22*(4), 639–682. https://doi.org/10.2307/2137804

Börsch-Supan, Axel. (2003). Labor market effects of population aging. *LABOUR, 17*(s1), 5–44. https://doi.org/10.1111/1467-9914.17.specialissue.2

Boserup, E. (1965). *The Conditions of Agricultural Progress*. Aldine Publishing Company, Chicago.

Boserup, E. (1981). *Population and Technological Change: A Study of Long-term Trends*. University of Chicago Press.

Boulding, K. E. (1956). General systems theory – the skeleton of science. *Management Science, 2*(3), 197–208.

Bradley, S. E., Croft, T. N., Fishel, J. D., & Westoff, C. F. (2012). *Revising Unmet Need for Family Planning* (DHS Analytical Studies No. 25). ICF International.

Burger, O., & DeLong, J. P. (2016). What if fertility decline is not permanent? The need for an evolutionary informed approach to understanding low fertility. *Philosophical Transactions of the Royal Society B: Biological Sciences, 371*(1692), 20150157. https://doi.org/10.1098/rstb.2015.0157

Butz, W. P., Lutz, W., & Sendzimir, J. (Eds.). (2014). *Education and Differential Vulnerability to Natural Disasters* (Special Issue, Ecology and Society, Vol. 19). Resilience Alliance. http://www.ecologyandsociety.org/issues/view.php?sf=73, http://www.iiasa.ac.at/publication/more_RP-14-001.php

Caldwell, J. C. (1980). Mass education as a determinant of the timing of fertility decline. *Population and Development Review, 6*(2), 225–255.

Caldwell, J. C. (2001). Demographers and the study of mortality. *Annals of the New York Academy of Sciences, 954*(1), 19–34. https://doi.org/10.1111/j.1749-6632.2001.tb02744.x

Caldwell, J. C. (2005). On net intergenerational wealth flows: An update. *Population and Development Review, 31*(4), 721–740.

Caldwell, J. C., & Caldwell, P. (1985). Education and literacy as factors in health. In S. B. Halstead, J. A. Walsh, & K. S. Warren (Eds.), *Good Health at Low Cost: Proceedings of a Conference Held at the Bellagio Conference Center*, Bellagio, Italy, April 29–May 3, 1985 (pp. 181–185). Rockefeller Foundation.

Caldwell, J. C., & Caldwell, P. (1986). *Limiting Population Growth and the Ford Foundation Contribution*. Pinter Publishers.

Cambridge Dictionary. (2020). Theory. In *Cambridge Dictionary*. Cambridge University Press. https://dictionary.cambridge.org/dictionary/english/theory

Caselli, G., Drefahl, S., Wegner-Siegmundt, C., & Luy, M. (2014). Future mortality in low mortality countries. In W. Lutz, W. P. Butz, & S. KC (Eds.), *World Population and Human Capital in the 21st Century* (pp. 226–272). Oxford University Press.

Chesnais, J.-C. (1992). *The Demographic Transition: Stages, Patterns, and Economic Implications*. Oxford University Press.

Clay, D. C., & Vander Haar, J. E. (1993). Patterns of intergenerational support and childbearing in the Third World. *Population Studies, 47*(1), 67–83. https://doi.org/10.1080/0032472031000146736

Coale, A. J. (1973). The demographic transition reconsidered. *Proceedings of the International Population Conference, 1*, 53–72.

Coale, A. J., & Hoover, E. M. (1958). *Population Growth and Economic Development in Low-income Countries: A Case Study of India's Prospects*. Princeton University Press.

Coale, A. J., & Trussell, T. J. (1974). Model fertility schedules: Variations in the age structure of childbearing in human populations. *Population Index, 40*(2), 185–258.

Coale, A. J., & Watkins, S. C. (1986). *The Decline of Fertility in Europe*. Princeton University Press.

Cochrane, S. H. (1979). *Fertility and Education. What Do We Really Know?* Johns Hopkins University Press.

Cochrane, S. H., Khan, A. M., & Osheba, I. K. T. (1990). Education, income, and desired fertility in Egypt: A revised perspective. *Economic Development and Cultural Change, 38*(2), 313–339.

Cohen, D., & Soto, M. (2007). Growth and human capital: Good data, good results. *Journal of Economic Growth, 12*(1), 51–76. https://doi.org/10.1007/s10887-007-9011-5

Cohen, J. E. (1996). *How Many People Can the Earth Support?* W. W. Norton & Company.

Coleman, D. (2006). Immigration and ethnic change in low-fertility countries: A third demographic transition. *Population and Development Review, 32*(3), 401–446.

Coleman, D., & Schofield, R. (1986). *The State of Population Theory: Forward from Malthus*. Blackwell Pub.

Coleman, J. S. (1987). Microfoundations and macrosocial behavior. In J. C. Alexander, B. Giesen, R. Munch, & N. J. Smelser (Eds.), *The Micro-Macro Link* (pp. 153–173). University of California Press.

Colgrove, J. (2002). The McKeown thesis: A historical controversy and its enduring influence. *American Journal of Public Health, 92*(5), 725–729. https://doi.org/10.2105/ajph.92.5.725

Condorcet, M. de. (1795). *Sketch for a Historical Picture of the Progress of the Human Mind*. Printed for J. Johnson.

Crespo Cuaresma, J., Lutz, W., & Sanderson, W. C. (2014). Is the demographic dividend an education dividend? *Demography, 51*(1), 299–315. https://doi.org/10.1007/s13524-013-0245-x

Cutler, D. M., Deaton, A., & Lleras-Muney, A. (2006). The determinants of mortality. *Journal of Economic Perspectives, 20*(3), 97–120. https://doi.org/10.1257/jep.20.3.97

Cutler, D. M., & Lleras-Muney, A. (2010). Understanding differences in health behaviors by education. *Journal of Health Economics, 29*(1), 1–28. https://doi.org/10.1016/j.jhealeco.2009.10.003

de la Fuente, A., & Doménech, R. (2006). Human capital in growth regressions: How much difference does data quality make? *Journal of the European Economic Association, 4*(1), 1–36. https://doi.org/10.1162/jeea.2006.4.1.1

Deaton, A. (2002). Policy implications of the gradient of health and wealth. *Health Affairs, 21*(2), 13–30. https://doi.org/10.1377/hlthaff.21.2.13

Defo, B. K. (1998). Fertility response to infant and child mortality in Africa with special reference to Cameroon. In M. R. Montgomery & B. Cohen (Eds.), *Death to Birth: Mortality Decline and Reproductive Change* (pp. 254–315). National Academies Press. https://www.ncbi.nlm.nih.gov/books/NBK233807/

Demeny, P. (1968). Early fertility decline in Austria-Hungary: A lesson in demographic transition. *Daedalus, 97*(2), 502–522.

Diekmann, A. (1995). *Empirische Sozialforschung: Grundlagen, Methoden, Anwendungen*. Rowohlt Taschenbuch Verlag.

Dilthey, W. (1900). *Die Entstehung der Hermeneutik [The Origin of Hermeneutics]* [Philosophische Abhandlungen, Festschrift für Christoph Sigwart]. J. C. B. Mohr (Paul Siebeck).

Easton, D. (1965). *A Systems Analysis of Political Life*. John Wiley & Sons.

Ehrlich, P. R. (1968). *The Population Bomb*. Ballantine. http://www.amazon.de/ The-Population-Bomb-Paul-Ehrlich/dp/1568495870

Elbert, T., Pantev, C., Wienbruch, C., Rockstroh, B., & Taub, E. (1995). Increased cortical representation of the fingers of the left hand in string players. *Science, 270*(5234), 305–307. https://doi.org/10.1126/science.270.5234.305

Erikson, R., & Goldthorpe, J. H. (2002). Intergenerational inequality: A sociological perspective. *The Journal of Economic Perspectives, 16*(3), 31–44.

Flinn, M. W. (1981). *European Demographic System, 1500–1820*. Johns Hopkins University Press.

Fogel, R. W. (1994). Economic growth, population theory, and physiology: The bearing of long-term processes on the making of economic policy. *The American Economic Review, 84*(3), 369–395.

Freese, J., & Lutfey, K. (2011). Fundamental causality: Challenges of an animating concept for medical sociology. In B. A. Pescosolido, J. K. Martin, J. D. McLeod, & A. Rogers (Eds.), *Handbook of the Sociology of Health, Illness, and Healing: A Blueprint for the 21st Century* (pp. 67–81). Springer. https://doi.org/10.1007/ 978-1-4419-7261-3_4

Frejka, T. (1996). Long-range global population projections: Lessons learned. In W. Lutz (Ed.), *The Future Population of the World. What Can We Assume Today?* (Revised Edition). Earthscan.

Fuchs, R., & Goujon, A. (2014). Future fertility in high fertility countries. In W. Lutz, W. P. Butz, & S. KC (Eds.), *World Population and Human Capital in the 21st Century* (pp. 147–225). Oxford University Press. http://ukcatalogue.oup .com/product/9780198703167.do

Galor, O. (2011). *Unified Growth Theory*. Princeton University Press.

Gietel-Basten, S., Lutz, W., & Scherbov, S. (2013). Very long range global population scenarios to 2300 and the implications of sustained low fertility. *Demographic Research, 28*(39), 1145–1166. https://doi.org/10.4054/DemRes .2013.28.39

Goujon, A., Lutz, W., & KC, S. (2015). Education stalls and subsequent stalls in African fertility: A descriptive overview. *Demographic Research, 33*(47), 1281–1296. https://doi.org/10.4054/DemRes.2015.33.47

Graunt, J. (1661). *Natural and Political Observations Made Upon the Bills of Mortality*.

Guha, S. (1994). The importance of social intervention in England's mortality decline: The evidence reviewed. *Social History of Medicine, 7*(1), 89–113. https://doi.org/10.1093/shm/7.1.89

Günther, E. (1931). Der Geburtenrückgang als Ursache der Arbeitslosigkeit? *Jahrbücher Für Nationalökonomie Und Statistik, 134*(1), 921–973. https://doi .org/10.1515/jbnst-1931-0187

Haines, M. R. (1998). The relationship between infant and child mortality and fertility: Some historical and contemporary evidence for the United States. In M. R. Montgomery & B. Cohen (Eds.), *Death to Birth: Mortality Decline and*

Reproductive Change (pp. 227–253). National Academies Press. https://www.ncbi.nlm.nih.gov/books/NBK233807/

Hajnal, J. (1965). European marriage patterns in perspective. In D. V. Glass & D. E. C. Eversley (Eds.), *Population in History. Essays in Historical Demography: Vol. Volume I: General and Great Britain* (pp. 101–143). Aldine Transaction.

Harris, B. (2004). Public health, nutrition, and the decline of mortality: The McKeown Thesis revisited. *Social History of Medicine, 17*(3), 379–407. https://doi.org/10.1093/shm/17.3.379

Hauser, P. M., & Duncan, O. D. (Eds.). (1959). *The Study of Population: An Inventory and Appraisal.* University of Chicago Press.

Henry, L. (1961). Some data on natural fertility. *Eugenics Quarterly, 8*(2), 81–91. https://doi.org/10.1080/19485565.1961.9987465

Högberg, U. (2004). The decline in maternal mortality in Sweden: The role of community midwifery. *American Journal of Public Health, 94*(8), 1312–1320. https://doi.org/10.2105/ajph.94.8.1312

Holling, C. S. (1973). Resilience and stability of ecological systems. *Annual Review of Ecology and Systematics, 4*(1), 1–23. https://doi.org/10.1146/annurev.es.04.110173.000245

Howell, N. (1979). *Demography of the Dobe !Kung.* Academic Press.

IIASA. (2014). *POPNET Newsletter* no. 45, p. 1. International Institute for Applied Systems Analysis.

Independent Group of Scientists appointed by the Secretary-General. (2019). *Global Sustainable Development Report 2019: The Future is Now – Science for Achieving Sustainable Development.* United Nations.

IPCC. (2014). *Climate Change 2014: Impacts, Adaptation, and Vulnerability. Part A: Global and Sectoral Aspects. Working Group II Contribution to the Fifth Assessment Report of the Intergovernmental Panel on Climate Change.* Cambridge University Press. http://www.ipcc.ch/pdf/assessment-report/ar5/wg2/WGIIAR5-FrontMatterA_FINAL.pdf

Jenkins, W. M., Merzenich, M. M., Ochs, M. T., Allard, T., & Guic-Robles, E. (1990). Functional reorganization of primary somatosensory cortex in adult owl monkeys after behaviorally controlled tactile stimulation. *Journal of Neurophysiology, 63*(1), 82–104. https://doi.org/10.1152/jn.1990.63.1.82

Johansson, E. (2007). The history of literacy in Sweden. In H. J. Graff (Ed.), *Literacy and Historical Development: A Reader* (pp. 238–271). Southern Illinois University Press.

Joshi, S., & Schultz, T. P. (2007). *Family Planning as an Investment in Development: Evaluation of a Program's Consequences in Matlab, Bangladesh* (IZA Discussion Papers No. 2639). Institute for the Study of Labor (IZA).

Kahneman, D. (2011). *Thinking, Fast and Slow* (8th edition). Farrar, Straus and Giroux.

Kandel, E. R. (2007). *In Search of Memory: The Emergence of a New Science of Mind.* W. W. Norton & Company.

Kaufmann, E. (2011). *Shall the Religious Inherit the Earth? Demography and Politics in the Twenty-First Century.* Profile Books.

KC, S., & Lentzner, H. (2010). The effect of education on adult mortality and disability: A global perspective. *Vienna Yearbook of Population Research, 8,* 201–235.

KC, S., Wurzer, M., Speringer, M., & Lutz, W. (2018). Future population and human capital in heterogeneous India. *Proceedings of the National Academy of Sciences, 115*(33), 8328–8333. https://doi.org/10.1073/pnas.1722359115

Kebede, E., Goujon, A., & Lutz, W. (2019). Stalls in Africa's fertility decline partly result from disruptions in female education. *Proceedings of the National Academy of Sciences, 116*(8), 2891–2896. https://doi.org/10.1073/pnas.1717288116

Kelley, A. C. (1988). Economic consequences of population change in the Third World. *Journal of Economic Literature, 26*(4), 1685–1728.

Kelley, A. C., & Schmidt, R. M. (1995). Aggregate population and economic growth correlations: The role of the components of demographic change. *Demography, 32*(4), 543–555.

Kelley, A. C., & Schmidt, R. M. (2005). Evolution of recent economic-demographic modeling: A synthesis. *Journal of Population Economics, 18*(2), 275–300. https://doi.org/10.1007/s00148-005-0222-9

Kenkel, D. S. (1991). Health behavior, health knowledge, and schooling. *Journal of Political Economy, 99*(2), 287–305. https://doi.org/10.1086/261751

Keyfitz, N. (1979). Multidimensionality in population analysis. In K. F. Schuessler (Ed.), *Sociological Methodology* (pp. 191–217). Jossey-Bass.

Keyfitz, N. (1982). Can knowledge improve forecasts? *Population and Development Review, 8*(4), 729–751. https://doi.org/10.2307/1972470

Keyfitz, N. (1984). Introduction: Biology and demography. In *Population and Biology* (pp. 1–7). Ordina and IUSSP.

Keyfitz, N. (1985). *Applied Mathematical Demography*. Springer.

Khan, H. T. A., & Lutz, W. (2008). How well did past UN population projections anticipate demographic trends in six south-east Asian countries? *Asian Population Studies, 4*(1), 77–95. https://doi.org/10.1080/17441730801966964

King, G. (1973). 17th century manuscript book of Gregory King. In *The Earliest Classics: Graunt and King* ([1696]). Gregg International.

Kirk, D. (1996). Demographic transition theory. *Population Studies, 50*(3), 361–387. https://doi.org/10.1080/0032472031000149536

Knibbs, S. G. H. (1976). *The Shadow of the World's Future, or, The Earth's Population Possibilities & the Consequences of the Present Rate of Increase of the Earth's Inhabitants* ([1928] Reprint Edition). Arno Press.

Kohler, H.-P. (2001). Fertility and social interaction: An economic perspective. In *Fertility and Social Interaction*. Oxford University Press. https://oxford.universitypressscholarship.com/view/10.1093/0199244596.001.0001/acprof-9780199244591

Kotschy, R., Urtaza, P. S., & Sunde, U. (2020). The demographic dividend is more than an education dividend. *Proceedings of the National Academy of Sciences, 117*(42), 25982–25984. https://doi.org/10.1073/pnas.2012286117

Kuznets, S. (1967). Population and economic growth. *Proceedings of the American Philosophical Society, 111*(3), 170–193.

Lakatos, I. (1978). *The Methodology of Scientific Research Programmes. Philosophical Papers Volume 1*. Cambridge University Press.

Landry, A. (1934). *La révolution démographique*. Sirey. https://academic.oup.com/ia/article/13/6/854/2704188

Lee, R. D. (1999). Probabilistic approaches to population forecasting. In W. Lutz, J. W. Vaupel, & D. A. Ahlburg (Eds.), *Frontiers of Population Forecasting* (pp. 156–190). Population Council.

Lee, R. D., & Mason, A. (2010). Some macroeconomic aspects of global population aging. *Demography, 47*, S151–S172.

Lee, R. D., & Mason, A. (Eds.). (2011). *Population Aging and the Generational Economy: A Global Perspective.* Edward Elgar Publishing.

Lee, R. D., & Mason, A. (2012). *Is Fertility Too Low? Capital, Transfers and Consumption.* Population Association of America.

Lee, R. D., Mason, A., & Miller, T. (2003). Saving, wealth and the transition from transfers to individual responsibility: The cases of Taiwan and the United States. *The Scandinavian Journal of Economics, 105*(3), 339–358. https://doi.org/10.1111/1467-9442.t01-2-00002

Leopoldina. (2019, July). *Brain Power for Sustainable Development: The Cognitive Preconditions for a Successful Sustainability Transition.* Brain Power for Sustainable Development, Berlin. https://www.leopoldina.org/uploads/tx_leopublication/2019_Statement_Brain_Power_web_01.pdf

Lesthaeghe, R. (1980). On the social control of human reproduction. *Population and Development Review, 6*(4), 527–548. https://doi.org/10.2307/1972925

Lesthaeghe, R. (2014). The second demographic transition: A concise overview of its development. *Proceedings of the National Academy of Sciences, 111*(51), 18112–18115. https://doi.org/10.1073/pnas.1420441111

Lindstrom, D. P., & Kiros, G.-E. (2007). The impact of infant and child death on subsequent fertility in Ethiopia. *Population Research and Policy Review, 26*(1), 31–49. https://doi.org/10.1007/s11113-006-9018-1

Link, B. G., & Phelan, J. (1995). Social conditions as fundamental causes of disease. *Journal of Health and Social Behavior*, 80–94. https://doi.org/10.2307/2626958

Luci-Greulich, A., & Thévenon, O. (2013). The impact of family policies on fertility trends in developed countries. *European Journal of Population/Revue Européenne de Démographie, 29*(4), 387–416. https://doi.org/10.1007/s10680-013-9295-4

Ludwig, A., Schelkle, T., & Vogel, E. (2012). Demographic change, human capital and welfare. *Review of Economic Dynamics, 15*(1), 94–107. https://doi.org/10.1016/j.red.2011.07.001

Lundberg, A. (2003). Living the transition – the great mortality change through the lives of the country doctors. *Interchange, 34*(2), 219–240. https://doi.org/10.1023/B:INCH.0000015902.92221.1e

Lutz, W. (1984). The changing nature of the link between infant mortality and fertility in Finland 1776–1978. *Finnish Yearbook of Population Research*, 26–45. https://doi.org/10.23979/fypr.44778

Lutz, W. (1987). *Finnish Fertility since 1722: Lessons from an Extended Decline.* Finnish Population Research Institute.

Lutz, W. (1989). *Distributional Aspects of Human Fertility: A Global Comparative Study.* Academic Press.

Lutz, W. (Ed.). (1994). *Population-Development-Environment: Understanding their interactions in Mauritius.* Springer Verlag. https://doi.org/10.1007/978-3-662-03061-5

Lutz, W. (2008). Has Korea's fertility reached the bottom? The hypothesis of a "Low Fertility Trap" in parts of Europe and East Asia. *Asian Population Studies*, 4(1), 1–4. https://doi.org/10.1080/17441730801963110

Lutz, W. (2009). *Toward a Systematic, Argument-Based Approach to Defining Assumptions for Population Projections* (Interim Report IR-09-037). IIASA. http://pure.iiasa.ac.at/id/eprint/9115/

Lutz, W. (2012). Identity sciences und intervention sciences: Was die Geistes- und Sozialwissenschaften leisten können. *Thema* (Austrian Academy of Sciences), 11, 3.

Lutz, W. (2013). Demographic metabolism: A predictive theory of socioeconomic change. *Population and Development Review*, 38, 283–301. https://doi.org/10.1111/j.1728-4457.2013.00564.x

Lutz, W. (2014a). A population policy rationale for the twenty-first century. *Population and Development Review*, 40(3), 527–544. https://doi.org/10.1111/j.1728-4457.2014.00696.x

Lutz, W. (2014b). The truth about aging populations. *Harvard Business Review*, 1, F1401E.

Lutz, W. (2015). Demographic metabolism: Enabling future generations. In B. Marin (Ed.), *The Future of Welfare in a Global Europe* (pp. 175–191). Ashgate.

Lutz, W. (2017a). Education empowers women to reach their personal fertility target, regardless of what the target is. *Vienna Yearbook of Population Research*, 15, 27–31. https://doi.org/10.1553/populationyearbook2017s027

Lutz, W. (2017b). Global Sustainable Development priorities 500 y after Luther: Sola schola et sanitate. *Proceedings of the National Academy of Sciences*, 114(27), 6904–6913. https://doi.org/10.1073/pnas.1702609114

Lutz, W. (2018). World population trends and the rise of homo sapiens literata. *Plenary Session of the Pontificial Academy of Sciences*, Casina Pio IV, November 12–14, 2018. Transformative Roles of Science in Society: From Emerging Basic Science toward Solutions for People's Wellbeing, Vatican City. http://www.pas.va/content/accademia/en/publications/acta/acta25/lutz.html

Lutz, W. (2020). Fertility will be determined by the changing ideal family size and the empowerment to reach these targets. *Vienna Yearbook of Population Research*, 18(2020), 1–8. https://doi.org/10.1553/populationyearbook2020.deb06

Lutz, W., Amran, G., Bélanger, A., Conte, A., Gailey, N., Ghio, D., Grapsa, E., Jensen, K., Loichinger, E., Marois, G., Muttarak, R., Potančoková, M., Sabourin, P., & Stonawski, M. (2019). *Demographic Scenarios for the EU – Migration, Population and Education*. Publications Office of the European Union.

Lutz, W., Butz, W. P., Castro, M., Dasgupta, P., Demeny, P. G., Ehrlich, I., Giorguli, S., Habte, D., Haug, W., Hayes, A., Herrmann, M., Jiang, L., King, D., Kotte, D., Lees, M., Makinwa-Adebusoye, P. K., McGranahan, G., Mishra, V., Montgomery, M. R., … Yeoh, B. (2012). Demography's role in sustainable development. *Science*, 335(6071), 918–918. https://doi.org/10.1126/science.335.6071.918-a

Lutz, W., Butz, W. P., & KC, S. (Eds.). (2014). *World Population and Human Capital in the 21st Century*. Oxford University Press.

Lutz, W., Crespo Cuaresma, J., & Abbasi-Shavazi, M. J. (2010). Demography, education, and democracy: Global trends and the case of Iran. *Population and*

Development Review, 36(2), 253–281. https://doi.org/10.1111/j.1728-4457.2010 .00329.x

Lutz, W., Crespo Cuaresma, J., & Gailey, N. (2019). The demographic dividend is driven by education, not changes in age structure. *NIUSSP*. https://www.niussp .org/article/the-demographic-dividend-is-driven-by-education/

Lutz, W., Crespo Cuaresma, J., Kebede, E., Prskawetz, A., Sanderson, W. C., & Striessnig, E. (2019). Education rather than age structure brings demographic dividend. *Proceedings of the National Academy of Sciences*, 116(26), 12798–12803. https://doi.org/10.1073/pnas.1820362116

Lutz, W., Crespo Cuaresma, J., & Sanderson, W. C. (2008). The demography of educational attainment and economic growth. *Science*, 319(5866), 1047–1048. https://doi.org/10.1126/science.1151753

Lutz, W., & Goldstein, J. R. (2004). Introduction: How to deal with uncertainty in population forecasting? *International Statistical Review*, 72(1), 1–4.

Lutz, W., Goujon, A., KC, S., & Sanderson, W. C. (2007). Reconstruction of populations by age, sex and level of educational attainment for 120 countries for 1970–2000. *Vienna Yearbook of Population Research*, 2007(5), 193–235.

Lutz, W., Goujon, A., KC, S., Stonawski, M., & Stilianakis, N. (Eds.). (2018). *Demographic and Human Capital Scenarios for the 21st Century*. Publications Office of the European Union.

Lutz, W., & KC, S. (2010). Dimensions of global population projections: What do we know about future population trends and structures? *Philosophical Transactions of the Royal Society of London. Series B, Biological Sciences*, 365(1554), 2779–2791. https://doi.org/10.1098/rstb.2010.0133

Lutz, W., & KC, S. (2011). Global human capital: Integrating education and population. *Science*, 333(6042), 587–592. https://doi.org/10.1126/science.1206964

Lutz, W., & Kebede, E. (2018). Education and health: Redrawing the Preston Curve. *Population and Development Review*, 44(2), 343–361. https://doi.org/ 10.1111/padr.12141

Lutz, W., Kritzinger, S., & Skirbekk, V. (2006). The demography of growing European identity. *Science*, 314(5798), 425–425. https://doi.org/10.1126/ science.1128313

Lutz, W., & Muttarak, R. (2017). Forecasting societies' adaptive capacities through a demographic metabolism model. *Nature Climate Change*, 7(3), 177–184. https://doi.org/10.1038/nclimate3222

Lutz, W., Muttarak, R., & Striessnig, E. (2014). Universal education is key to enhanced climate adaptation. *Science*, 346(6213), 1061–1062. https://doi.org/ 10.1126/science.1257975

Lutz, W., O'Neill, B. C., & Scherbov, S. (2003). Europe's population at a turning point. *Science*, 299(5615), 1991–1992. https://doi.org/10.1126/science.1080316

Lutz, W., Sanderson, W. C., & Scherbov, S. (2001). The end of world population growth. *Nature*, 412(6846), 543–545. https://doi.org/10.1038/35087589

Lutz, W., Sanderson, W. C., & Scherbov, S. (Eds.). (2004). *The End of World Population Growth in the 21st Century: New Challenges for Human Capital Formation and Sustainable Development*. Earthscan.

Lutz, W., Scherbov, S., & Volkov, A. (Eds.). (1993). *Demographic Trends and Patterns in the Soviet Union Before 1991*. Routledge.

Lutz, W., & Skirbekk, V. (2014). How education drives demography and knowledge informs projections. In W. Lutz, W. P. Butz, & S. KC (Eds.), *World Population and Human Capital in the 21st Century* (pp. 14–38). Oxford University Press.

Lutz, W., Skirbekk, V., & Testa, M. R. (2006). The low-fertility trap hypothesis: Forces that may lead to further postponement and fewer births in Europe. *Vienna Yearbook of Population Research, 4,* 167–192.

Lutz, W., Striessnig, E., Dimitrov, A., Ghisland, S., Lijad, A., Reiter, C., Spitzer, S., & Yildiz, D. (2021). Years of Good Life (YoGL): A wellbeing indicator designed to serve research on sustainability. *Proceedings of the National Academy of Sciences, forthcoming.*

Lutz, W., Vaupel, J. W., & Ahlburg, D. A. (1999). *Frontiers of Population Forecasting.* Population Council.

Lyons, M. (2001). The new readers of nineteenth-century France. In M. Lyons (Ed.), *Readers and Society in Nineteenth-Century France: Workers, Women, Peasants* (pp. 1–16). Palgrave Macmillan UK. https://doi.org/10.1057/9780230287808_1

Mackenbach, J. P. (2019). *Health Inequalities: Persistence and Change in European Welfare States.* Oxford University Press.

Malthus, T. R. (1798). *An Essay on the Principle of Population.* J. Johnson.

Mankiw, N. G., Romer, D., & Weil, D. N. (1992). A contribution to the empirics of economic growth. *Quarterly Journal of Economics, 107*(2), 407–437. https://doi.org/10.2307/2118477

Mannheim, K. (1952). The problem of generations. In P. Kecskemeti (Ed.), *Essays on the Sociology of Knowledge by Karl Mannheim.* Routledge & Kegan Paul.

Manton, K. G. (1988). A longitudinal study of functional change and mortality in the United States. *Journal of Gerontology, 43*(5), S153–S161. https://doi.org/10.1093/geronj/43.5.S153

Marois, G., Bélanger, A., & Lutz, W. (2020). Population aging, migration, and productivity in Europe. *Proceedings of the National Academy of Sciences, 117*(14), 7690–7695. https://doi.org/10.1073/pnas.1918988117

Marois, G., Sabourin, P., & Bélanger, A. (2019a). Forecasting human capital of EU member countries accounting for sociocultural determinants. *Journal of Demographic Economics, 85*(3), 231–269.

Marois, G., Sabourin, P., & Bélanger, A. (2019b). Implementing dynamics of immigration integration in labor force participation projection in EU28. *Population Research and Policy Review.* https://doi.org/10.1007/s11113-019-09537-y

Mårtensson, J., Eriksson, J., Bodammer, N. C., Lindgren, M., Johansson, M., Nyberg, L., & Lövdén, M. (2012). Growth of language-related brain areas after foreign language learning. *NeuroImage, 63*(1), 240–244. https://doi.org/10.1016/j.neuroimage.2012.06.043

Marx, K. (2002). Grundrisse: Foundations of the critique of political economy. *Readings in Economic Sociology,* 18–23.

Maslow, A. H. (1954). *Motivation and Personality.* Harper & Brothers.

Mason, A., & Lee, R. D. (2006). Reform and support systems for the elderly in developing countries: Capturing the second demographic dividend. *Genus, 62*(2), 11–35.

Mason, A., & Lee, R. D. (2007). Transfers, capital, and consumption over the demographic transition. In R. Clark, N. Ogawa, & A. Mason (Eds.), *Population Aging, Intergenerational Transfers and the Macroeconomy* (pp. 128–162). Edward Elgar.

Matthews, K. A., Gallo, L. C., & Taylor, S. E. (2010). Are psychosocial factors mediators of socioeconomic status and health connections? A progress report and blueprint for the future. *Annals of the New York Academy of Sciences, 1186,* 146–173. https://doi.org/10.1111/j.1749-6632.2009.05332.x

May, J. F. (2012). *World Population Policies: Their Origin, Evolution, and Impact.* Springer. https://doi.org/10.1007/978-94-007-2837-0

Mazzuco, S., & Keilman, N. (Eds.). (2020). *Developments in Demographic Forecasting.* Springer.

McDonald, P. (2000). Gender equity in theories of fertility transition. *Population and Development Review, 26*(3), 427–439.

McKeown, R. E. (2009). The epidemiologic transition: Changing patterns of mortality and population dynamics. *American Journal of Lifestyle Medicine.* https://doi.org/10.1177/1559827609335350

McKeown, T. (1976). *The Modern Rise of Population.* Academic Press.

Meadows, D., Meadows, D., Randers, J., & Behrens, W. W. I. (1972). *The Limits to Growth.* Universe Books.

Mechanic, D. (2007). Population health: Challenges for science and society. *The Milbank Quarterly, 85,* 533–559. https://doi.org/10.1111/j.1468-0009.2007.00498.x

Meijer, W. A., Boxtel, M. P. J. van, Gerven, P. W. M. V., Hooren, S. A. H. van, & Jolles, J. (2009). Interaction effects of education and health status on cognitive change: A 6-year follow-up of the Maastricht Aging Study. *Aging & Mental Health, 13*(4), 521–529. https://doi.org/10.1080/13607860902860821

Mill, J. S. (1848). Principles of political economy. In Appleman, P. (Ed.) 1976, *An Essay on the Principle of Population, Thomas Robert Malthus* (pp. 151–156). Norton.

Ministerium für Schule und Weiterbildung. (2012). *Ministerin Löhrmann: "Bildungspolitik ist die Wirtschafts- und Sozialpolitik des 21. Jahrhunderts"* [Press Release]. Ministerium für Schule und Weiterbildung. http://www.schulministerium.nrw.de/docs/bp/Ministerium/Presse/Pressemitteilungen/2012_-16_-Legislaturperiode/PM20120614/index.html

Mirowsky, J., & Ross, C. E. (2003). *Education, Social Status, and Health.* Aldine de Gruyter.

Molina, M. G. de, & Toledo, V. M. (2014). *The Social Metabolism: A Socio-ecological Theory of Historical Change.* Springer International Publishing. https://doi.org/10.1007/978-3-319-06358-4

MPIDR. (2008, April 23). *Births, Deaths, and Mathematics* [Press release]. Max Planck Institute for Demographic Research. https://www.demogr.mpg.de/de/news_events_6123/news_pressemitteilungen_4630/presse/_births_deaths_and_mathematics_1392

Murphy, M., & O'Leary, E. (2010). Depression, cognitive reserve and memory performance in older adults. *International Journal of Geriatric Psychiatry, 25*(7), 665–671. https://doi.org/10.1002/gps.2404

Murtin, F. (2013). Long-term determinants of the demographic transition, 1870–2000. *The Review of Economics and Statistics, 95*(2), 617–631.

Nakicenovic, N., Alcamo, J., Grubler, A., Riahi, K., Roehrl, R. A., Rogner, H.-H., & Victor, N. (2000). *Special Report on Emissions Scenarios (SRES), A Special Report of Working Group III of the Intergovernmental Panel on Climate Change.* Cambridge University Press. http://pure.iiasa.ac.at/id/eprint/6101/

National Research Council. (1986). *Population Growth and Economic Development: Policy Questions.* National Academy Press.

National Research Council. (2001). *Diffusion Processes and Fertility Transition: Selected Perspectives.* The National Academies Press. https://doi.org/10.17226/10228

Nelson, R. R., & Phelps, E. S. (1966). Investment in humans, technological diffusion, and economic growth. *The American Economic Review, 56*(1/2), 69–75.

Nerlove, M., Razin, A., & Sadka, E. (1987). *Population Policy and Individual Choice: A Theoretical Investigation.* International Food Policy Research Institute.

Notestein, F. W. (1944). *The Future Population of Europe and the Soviet Union: Population Projections, 1940–1970.* League of Nations.

Notestein, F. W. (1945). Population – The long view. In T. W. Schultz (Ed.), *Food for the World.* University of Chicago Press.

Notestein, F. W. (1953). Economic problems of population change. *Proceedings of the Eighth International Conference of Agricultural Economists,* 13–31.

Olshansky, S. J., Antonucci, T., Berkman, L., Binstock, R. H., Boersch-Supan, A., Cacioppo, J. T., Carnes, B. A., Carstensen, L. L., Fried, L. P., & Goldman, D. P. (2012). Differences in life expectancy due to race and educational differences are widening, and many may not catch up. *Health Affairs, 31*(8), 1803–1813. https://doi.org/10.1377/hlthaff.2011.0746

Omran, A. R. (1971). The epidemiologic transition: A theory of the epidemiology of population change. *Milbank Quarterly, 39*(4, Pt. 1), 509–538. https://doi.org/10.2307/3349375

O'Neill, B. C. (2004). Conditional probabilistic population projections: An application to climate change. *International Statistical Review/Revue Internationale de Statistique, 72*(2), 167–184.

O'Neill, B. C., Dalton, M., Fuchs, R., Jiang, L., Pachauri, S., & Zigova, K. (2010). Global demographic trends and future carbon emissions. *Proceedings of the National Academy of Sciences, 107,* 17521–17526. https://doi.org/10.1073/pnas.1004581107

Pamuk, E. R., Fuchs, R., & Lutz, W. (2011). Comparing relative effects of education and economic resources on infant mortality in developing countries. *Population and Development Review, 37*(4), 637–664.

Pearl, J. (2000). *Causality: Models, Reasoning and Inference.* Cambridge University Press.

Pearl, R. (1923). *The Rate of Living.* Alfred Knopf.

Pearl, R. (1924). *Studies in Human Biology.* Williams & Wilkins.

Popper, K. (1959). *The Logic of Scientific Discovery.* Basic Books.

Potančoková, M., & Marois, G. (2020). Projecting future births with fertility differentials reflecting women's educational and migrant characteristics. *Vienna Yearbook of Population Research, 18,* 1–26. https://doi.org/10.1553/populationyearbook2020.res02

Preston, S. H. (1975). The changing relation between mortality and level of economic development. *Population Studies, 29*(2), 231–248. https://doi.org/10.2307/2173509

Preston, S. H., & Coale, A. J. (1982). Age structure, growth, attrition, and accession: A new synthesis. *Population Index, 48*(2), 217–259. https://doi.org/10.2307/2735961

Preston, S. H., Heuveline, P., & Guillot, M. (2000). *Demography: Measuring and Modeling Population Processes* (1st Edition). Wiley-Blackwell.

Pritchett, L. (2001). Where has all the education gone? *The World Bank Economic Review, 15*(3), 367–391. https://doi.org/10.1093/wber/15.3.367

Prskawetz, A., Fent, T., Barthel, W., Crespo-Cuaresma, J., Lindh, T., Malmberg, B., & Halvarsson, M. (2007). *The Relationship between Demographic Change and Economic Growth in the EU* (Forschungsbericht Report for Tender VT/2005/035). Austrian Academy of Sciences (ÖAW), Vienna Institute of Demography (VID). https://www.oeaw.ac.at/fileadmin/subsites/Institute/VID/PDF/Publications/Forschungsberichte/FB32.pdf

Prskawetz, A., & Hammer, B. (2019). Does education matter? – Economic dependency ratios by education. In *Vienna Yearbook of Population Research* (Vol. 16, pp. 1–24). Verlag der Österreichischen Akademie der Wissenschaften. https://www.austriaca.at/0xc1aa5576%200x003a1454.pdf

Prskawetz, A., & Sambt, J. (2014). Economic support ratios and the demographic dividend in Europe. *Demographic Research, 30*, 963–1010. https://doi.org/10.4054/DemRes.2014.30.34

Rees, P., van der Gaag, N., de Beer, J., & Heins, F. (2012). European regional populations: current trends, future pathways, and policy options. *European Journal of Population/Revue Européenne de Démographie, 28*(4), 385–416. https://doi.org/10.1007/s10680-012-9268-z

Reis, J. (2005). Economic growth, human capital formation and consumption in Western Europe before 1800. In R. C. Allen, T. Bengtsson, & M. Dribe (Eds.), *Living Standards in the Past: New Perspectives on Well-Being in Asia and Europe* (pp. 195–226). Oxford University Press. https://doi.org/10.1093/0199280681.003.0009

Richards, M., & Hatch, S. L. (2011). Good news about the ageing brain. *BMJ, 343*. https://doi.org/10.1136/bmj.d6288

Rogers, A. (1975). *Introduction to Multiregional Mathematical Demography*. Wiley.

Rogers, A. (1995). Population forecasting: Do simple models outperform complex models? *Mathematical Population Studies, 5*(3), 187–202. https://doi.org/10.1080/08898489509525401

Ryder, N. B. (1965). The cohort as a concept in the study of social change. *American Sociological Review, 30*(6), 843–861. https://doi.org/10.2307/2090964

Sanderson, W. C., & Scherbov, S. (2005). Average remaining lifetimes can increase as human populations age. *Nature, 435*(7043), 811–813. https://doi.org/10.1038/nature03593

Sanderson, W. C., & Scherbov, S. (2010). Remeasuring aging. *Science, 329*(5997), 1287–1288. https://doi.org/10.1126/science.1193647

Sanderson, W. C., Scherbov, S., Lutz, W., & O'Neill, B. C. (2004). Applications of probabilistic population forecasting. In W. Lutz, W. C. Sanderson, & S.

Scherbov (Eds.), *The End of World Population Growth in the 21st Century: New Challenges for Human Capital Formation and Sustainable Development* (pp. 85–120). Earthscan.

Sandström, G., Kebede, E., & Lutz, W. (2016). Child mortality and education in Sweden as derived from the POPLINK mortality data base 1800–1929 [Unpublished manuscript]. Vienna Institute for Demography of the Austrian Academy of Sciences.

Sauvy, A. (1969). *General Theory of Population* (English version). Basic Books.

Schoen, R., & Nelson, V. E. (1974). Marriage, divorce, and mortality: A life table analysis. *Demography, 11*(2), 267–290. https://doi.org/10.2307/2060563

Schofield, R. (1984). Population growth in the century after 1750: The role of mortality decline. In T. Bengtsson, G. Fridlizius, & R. Ohlsson (Eds.), *Pre-Industrial Population Change: The Mortality Decline and Short-Term Population Movements* (pp. 17–39). Almquist & Wiksell International.

Schofield, R., & Reher, D. S. (1991). The decline of mortality in Europe. In R. Schofield, D. S. Reher, & A. Bideau (Eds.), *The Decline of Mortality in Europe*. Clarendon Press.

Shalem, M. (2018). *Total Fertility Trends in Israel*. The Institute for Zionist Strategies. https://www.izs.org.il/2018/08/total-fertility-trends-israel

Shapiro, D., & Gebreselassie, T. (2008). Fertility transition in Sub-Saharan Africa: Falling and stalling. *African Population Studies, 23*(1), Article 1. https://doi.org/10.11564/23-1-310

Sibly, R. M., Hone, J., & Clutton-Brock, T. H. (Eds.). (2003). *Wildlife Population Growth Rates*. The Royal Society in association with Cambridge University Press.

Simon, J. L. (1981). *The Ultimate Resource*. Princeton University Press.

Sinding, S. W. (2005). Why is funding for population activities declining? *Asia-Pacific Population Journal, 20*(2), 3–9. https://doi.org/10.18356/be7b6c98-en

Skirbekk, V. (2008). Fertility trends by social status. *Demographic Research, 18*(5), 145–180. https://doi.org/10.4054/DemRes.2008.18.5

Skirbekk, V., Stonawski, M., & Alfani, G. (2014). *Global and Regional Population Growth if European Demographic Transition Patterns Had Been Universal* (Interim Report IR-14-014). IIASA. http://pure.iiasa.ac.at/id/eprint/11253/

Smil, V. (2005). The Next 50 Years: Fatal discontinuities. *Population and Development Review, 31*(2), 201–236. https://doi.org/10.1111/j.1728-4457.2005.00063.x

Smith, J. P. (2007). The impact of socioeconomic status on health over the life-course. *The Journal of Human Resources, 42*(4), 739–764.

Sobotka, T., & Beaujouan, É. (2014). Two is best? The persistence of a two-child family ideal in Europe. *Population and Development Review, 40*(3), 391–419. https://doi.org/10.1111/j.1728-4457.2014.00691.x

Sobotka, T., & Lutz, W. (2010). Misleading policy messages derived from the period TFR: Should we stop using it? *Comparative Population Studies, 35*(3), Article 3. https://doi.org/10.12765/CPoS-2010-15

Solow, R. M. (1956). A contribution to the theory of economic growth. *The Quarterly Journal of Economics, 70*(1), 65–94. https://doi.org/10.2307/1884513

Srinivasan, T. N. (1988). Population growth and economic development. *Journal of Policy Modeling, 10*(1), 7–28.

Stone, L. (2020, March 5). Pro-natal policies work, but they come with a hefty price tag. *Institute for Family Studies.* https://ifstudies.org/blog/pro-natal -policies-work-but-they-come-with-a-hefty-price-tag

Striessnig, E., & Lutz, W. (2013). Can below-replacement fertility be desirable? *Empirica, 40*(3), 409–425. https://doi.org/10.1007/s10663-013-9213-3

Striessnig, E., & Lutz, W. (2014). How does education change the relationship between fertility and age dependency under environmental constraints? A long-term simulation exercise. *Demographic Research, 30*, 465–492. doi:10 .4054/DemRes.2014.30.16.

Striessnig, E., & Lutz, W. (2016). Demographic strengthening of European identity. *Population and Development Review,* online version: 2 June. doi: 10.1111/j.1728-4457.2016.00133.x.

Sundbärg, G. (1907). *Bevölkerungsstatistik Schwedens, 1750–1900.* Norstedt. https://catalog.hathitrust.org/Record/100347621

Süssmilch, J. P. (1741). *Die Göttliche Ordnung in den Veränderungen des menschlichen Geschlechts aus der Geburt, dem Tode und der Fortpflanzung desselben [The Divine Order with Regard to the Human Species, as Demonstrated by Birth, Death and Reproduction].* Daniel August Gohls.

Swan, T. W. (1956). Economic growth and capital accumulation. *Economic Record, 32*(2), 334–361. https://doi.org/10.1111/j.1475-4932.1956.tb00434.x

Szreter, S. (1988). The importance of social intervention in Britain's mortality decline c.1850–1914: A re-interpretation of the role of public health. *Social History of Medicine, 1*(1), 1–38. https://doi.org/10.1093/shm/1.1.1

The World Bank. (2020). *GDP per Capita (Constant 2010 US$)—Cuba.* The World Bank. https://data.worldbank.org/indicator/NY.GDP.PCAP.KD ?locations=CU

Thompson, W. S. (1929). Population. *American Journal of Sociology, 34*(6), 959–975.

Thornton, A. (2005). *Reading History Sideways: The Fallacy and Enduring Impact of the Developmental Paradigm on Family Life* (1st Edition). University of Chicago Press.

UNDP. (2013). *Human Development Report 2013: The Rise of the South: Human Progress in a Diverse World.* United Nations Development Programme. http:// www.undp.org/content/dam/undp/library/corporate/HDR/2013GlobalHDR/ English/HDR2013%20Report%20English.pdf

UNFPA. (2020, July 8). *UNFPA Demographic Resilience Programme for Europe and Central Asia.* UNFPA EECA. https://eeca.unfpa.org/en/demographic -resilience

United Nations. (2001). *Replacement Migration: Is It a Solution to Declining and Ageing Populations?* United Nations, Department of Economic and Social Affairs, Population Division. http://www.un.org/esa/population/publications/ migration/migration.htm

United Nations. (2019). *World Population Prospects: The 2019 Revision.* Department of Economic and Social Affairs, Population Division. http://esa .un.org/unpd/wpp/

University of Oxford. (2020). *Social Policy and Intervention*. https://www.ox.ac.uk/ admissions/graduate/courses/social-sciences/social-policy-and-intervention

Vallin, J., & Meslé, F. (2004). Convergences and divergences in mortality: A new approach of health transition. *Demographic Research, S2*, 11–44. https://doi .org/10.4054/DemRes.2004.S2.2

van de Walle, E. (1992). Fertility transition, conscious choice, and numeracy. *Demography, 29*(4), 487–502. https://doi.org/10.2307/2061848

van de Walle, F. (1980). Education and the demographic transition in Switzerland. *Population and Development Review, 6*(3), 463–472. https://doi.org/10.2307/ 1972411

van der Pol, M. (2011). Health, education and time preference. *Health Economics, 20*(8), 917–929. https://doi.org/10.1002/hec.1655

Vaupel, J. W., & Yashin, A. I. (1985). Heterogeneity's ruses: Some surprising effects of selection on population dynamics. *The American Statistician, 39*(3), 176–185. https://doi.org/10.2307/2683925

VID, & IIASA. (2020). *European Demographic Datasheet 2020*. Wittgenstein Centre for Demography and Global Human Capital. www.populationeurope .org

Vishnevsky, A. (1991). Demographic revolution and the future of fertility: A systems approach. In W. Lutz (Ed.), *Future Demographic Trends in Europe and North America: What Can We Assume Today?* (pp. 257–270). Academic Press.

Watkins, S. C. (1986). Conclusions. In A. J. Coale & S. C. Watkins (Eds.), *The Decline of Fertility in Europe* (pp. 420–450). Princeton University Press.

Weeks, J. R. (2014). *Population: An Introduction to Concepts and Issues*. Wadsworth Publishing.

Weitzman, A. (2017). The effects of women's education on maternal health: Evidence from Peru. *Social Science & Medicine, 180*, 1–9. https://doi.org/10 .1016/j.socscimed.2017.03.004

WIC. (2018). *Wittgenstein Centre Data Explorer Version 2.0 (Beta)*. Wittgenstein Centre for Demography and Global Human Capital (IIASA, University of Vienna, VID/OeAW). www.wittgensteincentre.org/dataexplorer

Willekens, F. (1978). *The Demography of Labor Force Participation* (IIASA Research Memorandum RM-78-017). IIASA. http://pure.iiasa.ac.at/id/eprint/ 980/

Willekens, F. J. (1999). The life course: Models and analysis. In L. J. G. van Wissen & P. A. Dykstra (Eds.), *Population Issues: An Interdisciplinary Focus* (pp. 23–51). Springer Netherlands. https://doi.org/10.1007/978-94-011-4389 -9_2

Wright, G. H. von. (1971). *Explanation and Understanding*. Cornell University Press.

Index

Titles in the **Elgar Advanced Introductions** series include:

International Political Economy
Benjamin J. Cohen

The Austrian School of Economics
Randall G. Holcombe

Cultural Economics
Ruth Towse

Law and Development
Michael J. Trebilcock and Mariana Mota Prado

International Humanitarian Law
Robert Kolb

International Trade Law
Michael J. Trebilcock

Post Keynesian Economics
J.E. King

International Intellectual Property
Susy Frankel and Daniel J. Gervais

Public Management and Administration
Christopher Pollitt

Organised Crime
Leslie Holmes

Nationalism
Liah Greenfeld

Social Policy
Daniel Béland and Rianne Mahon

Globalisation
Jonathan Michie

Entrepreneurial Finance
Hans Landström

International Conflict and Security Law
Nigel D. White

Comparative Constitutional Law
Mark Tushnet

International Human Rights Law
Dinah L. Shelton

Entrepreneurship
Robert D. Hisrich

International Tax Law
Reuven S. Avi-Yonah

Public Policy
B. Guy Peters

The Law of International Organizations
Jan Klabbers

International Environmental Law
Ellen Hey

International Sales Law
Clayton P. Gillette

Corporate Venturing
Robert D. Hisrich

Public Choice
Randall G. Holcombe

Private Law
Jan M. Smits

Consumer Behavior Analysis
Gordon Foxall

Behavioral Economics
John F. Tomer

Cost-Benefit Analysis

Ken Conca

Business Ethics
John Hooker

Employee Engagement
Alan M. Saks and Jamie A. Gruman

Governance
Jon Pierre and B. Guy Peters

Demography
Wolfgang Lutz